PLANTS & GARDENS

BROOKLYN BOTANIC GARDEN RECORD

GREENHOUSES
& GARDEN ROOMS

1990

Brooklyn Botanic Garden

STAFF FOR THE ORIGINAL EDITION:

TOVAH MARTIN, GUEST EDITOR

BARBARA B. PESCH, EDITOR

JO KEIM, ASSOCIATE EDITOR

STAFF FOR THE REVISED EDITION:

BARBARA B. PESCH, DIRECTOR OF PUBLICATIONS

JANET MARINELLI, ASSOCIATE EDITOR

AND THE EDITORIAL COMMITTEE OF THE BROOKLYN BOTANIC GARDEN

BEKKA LINDSTROM, ART DIRECTOR

JUDITH D. ZUK, PRESIDENT, BROOKLYN BOTANIC GARDEN

ELIZABETH SCHOLTZ, DIRECTOR EMERITUS, BROOKLYN BOTANIC GARDEN

STEPHEN K-M. TIM, VICE PRESIDENT, SCIENCE & PUBLICATIONS

COVER PHOTOGRAPH BY ELVIN MCDONALD
ALL PHOTOGRAPHS BY ELVIN MCDONALD, EXCEPT WHERE NOTED

Plants & Gardens, Brooklyn Botanic Garden Record (ISSN 0362-5850) is published quarterly at 1000 Washington Ave., Brooklyn, N.Y. 11225, by the **Brooklyn Botanic Garden, Inc.** Second-class-postage paid at Brooklyn, N.Y., and at additional mailing offices. Subscription included in Botanic Garden membership dues ($25.00) per year). Copyright © 1988, 1990 by the Brooklyn Botanic Garden, Inc.

PLANTS & GARDENS

BROOKLYN BOTANIC GARDEN RECORD

GREENHOUSES & GARDEN ROOMS

THIS HANDBOOK IS A REVISED EDITION OF PLANTS & GARDENS, VOL. 44, No. 2

HANDBOOK # 116

A section of the orchid collection at Golden Gate Park Conservatory is displayed with ferns.

F O R E W O R D

Tovah Martin

or people who love plants, one of life's pleasures is to provide their collection with the perfect environment. Sometimes, ideal conditions are available outdoors. But, when this is not the case, gardeners turn to greenhouses and garden rooms to furnish the warmth, light and humidity that plants require.

Many gardeners dream of having a greenhouse. And that goal becomes increasingly easy to achieve as greenhouse technology advances and more systems appear on the market. Greenhouses come in all shapes and sizes. They can be added to the window of a city apartment or stand separate from the house. There is a greenhouse for every gardener.

Our goal in this handbook is to introduce you to the various types of greenhouses and garden rooms and to help you choose which is appropriate to your purposes. We have described some of the mechanical workings of a greenhouse so that you can heat, cool, ventilate and shade your structure efficiently. And, knowing that many of you are planning to grow a specific crop in your greenhouses, we have described greenhouses for cut flowers, orchids, winter-forced bulbs, and cool-loving plants. This handbook also presents ideas for plant maintenance in the greenhouse environment. Finally, because problems will occur, we have covered pest and disease management in the greenhouse. 🌱

THE GREENHOUSE'S ROOTS

TOVAH MARTIN

Greenhouses are not modern inventions. There is written evidence that the Romans fashioned transparent structures for the protection of rare, tender fruit off-season. Those buildings were called *specularia* and they were glazed with thin sheets of talc and mica. In addition, they were heated by amazingly sophisticated stove and flue systems.

Although artificial environments for protecting plants against the elements have had many critics over the centuries, man has continued to build and to perfect glass structures. In the 17th century, *orangeries* came into vogue in Europe. These glass-sided buildings were constructed specifically to protect citrus, the fruit of kings, thus allowing royalty the luxury of enjoying juicy sweet fruit off-season. However, *orangeries* were heated either by primitive stoves that required constant attention or by steaming manure piles.

With the dawning of the 19th century, greenhouse technology took flight. In 1845 excise taxes on glass were lifted. Before long glass-making processes were revamped, making glass inexpensive, readily available and of good quality. At the same time tropical plants were arriving in Europe from the temperate regions of the globe. Gardeners struggled to develop glass structures that were sufficiently sophisticated to shelter this

magnificent tropical plant life. They set to work studying slopes, calculating positions, as well as inventing efficient furnaces and piping systems. Greenhouse construction took a giant leap forward.

But greenhouses were expensive to construct and maintain. That situation was not destined to change overnight. Finally, by the middle of the 19th century, prefabricated greenhouses appeared. They were common on the European market by the 1880s.

In North America, we have some unique environmental problems with which to contend — for one, a severer winter climate than in Great Britain. Throughout most of the 19th Century, we trailed behind Europe in the construction of greenhouses. Finally, Frederic A. Lord happened upon the scene. Lord built his first greenhouse in the frigid city of Buffalo in the mid-1850s and from then on he labored to perfect stoves that would maintain greenhouse temperatures despite sub-zero outdoor temperatures. Apparently, he was successful. By the 1870s, his greenhouse building business was so brisk that Lord took his son-in-law, William Burnham, into partnership.

We've come a long way since those early greenhouses and we undoubtedly have a good distance to travel until greenhouse technology has reached its pinnacle. However, we owe a debt of gratitude to the first gardener who decided that he must have fruit despite the weather outdoors. 🍎

TOVAH MARTIN *is staff horticulturist at Logee's Greenhouses and the author of* **Once Upon a Windowsill** *published by Timber Press, 1988.*

SELECTING A HOBBY GREENHOUSE

John W. Bartok, Jr.

A hobby greenhouse will allow you to enjoy gardening when the weather outside is too cold for growing plants. When deciding on a greenhouse an important consideration is how it will be operated.

The season-extender greenhouse is used primarily to extend the growing season by a few weeks in the spring and fall. Garden vegetables and bedding plants can be started earlier in the spring and flowering plants kept in bloom later in the fall.

For year-round operation some supplemental heat is needed. If a cool greenhouse is operated to grow leafy vegetables or overwinter ornamental shrubs, it can be a small auxiliary heater. For most flowering plants a system capable of optimum temperatures is needed.

A greenhouse or sunspace attached to the house can be used as an extension of the living space or as a solar collector if designed properly. An orientation to the south is preferred. If operated as a greenhouse it has the advantages of convenient access and nearness to water and electricity.

Freestanding greenhouses are generally more expensive but allow greater flexibility than attached styles because

John W. Bartok Jr., *Storrs, CT is an extension professor and extension agricultural engineer at the University of Connecticut. He is also a monthly columnist on greenhouse construction and maintenance for* **Horticulture** *magazine and* **Greenhouse Manager** *and has authored or coauthored four books, the most recent being* **Greenhouse Engineering***.*

they can be larger and located to receive more sunlight. Many different shapes are available.

The pit greenhouse, built partially below ground, uses the earth to keep it cool during the summer and warm during the winter. Strong walls to withstand the soil pressure and adequate floor drains are needed.

Size

Usually available space and cost, more than need or desire, dictate greenhouse size. When choosing a size, ask yourself how you will use the greenhouse. Are you really an avid gardener that has the time to care for the plants. If you are only starting a few seedlings for the summer garden, perhaps a hotbed is a better choice.

A minimum size for a hobby greenhouse is 8'x12' or 10'x10'. This gives enough room for benches and a work aisle. Eave height of gable-roof houses should be at least five and one-half feet and ridge height at least eight feet.

Frame and Foundation

Aluminum or galvanized metal frames are attractive and require little maintenance. To reduce heat loss some metal frames have thermal breaks. A wood frame is often the first choice of the do-it-yourselfer. Wood is easy to work with and costs less than other materials. Pressure-treated material should be used where it is in contact with the ground or for benches. It will last 25 years or more.

An attached greenhouse opening into the house can become a garden room — a space for people as well as plants. PHOTO BY GEORGE TALOUMIS

Do not use wood treated with creosote or pentachlorophenol because it releases vapors harmful to plants.

Plans for wood frame hobby greenhouses are available from the Agricultural Extension Engineer at your Land Grant University. If you own and like to use a few basic hand tools, you may want to purchase a greenhouse kit. All the materials for the structure except the foundation are usually included. The names of local greenhouse suppliers can be found in the phone book business pages.

All greenhouses should be anchored to a solid, level foundation. Concrete, concrete block or brick are commonly used. Pressure treated posts set 18 inches or more in soil or concrete make a simple, low-cost foundation for a wood frame greenhouse.

Several inches of gravel or pea stone should be used on the floor for drainage. Brick, flagstones or concrete make a good walkway.

Benches and Beds

Benches raise the plants to a convenient working height. A standard height is 30-32 inches. Side benches should be two or three feet wide and center benches may be as wide as six feet. Growing beds can be built as movable boxes or fixed permanently to the greenhouse floor. Frequently a ground-bed is located along the south sidewall to reduce shading of plants in the rest of the house. Pipes or wires above benches can hold hanging plants.

Glazing

Of primary importance in growing plants is the amount of light energy available for photosynthesis. This is especially true in northern latitudes during the winter when the sun angle is low and the daylength is short.

Glass is still the most common glazing for hobby greenhouses. Its clean appearance and transparency adapt well to today's homes. With larger panes available (up to four feet by seven feet) more light gets into the greenhouse. Low-cost tempered sliding-glass-door replacement panes make excellent glazing for custom built greenhouses. Bar caps and strip caulking material have reduced installation labor. The use of double wall tempered glass reduces heat loss by about one third. The additional cost of low iron glass is usually not cost effective even though light levels are increased by two to three percent.

Polycarbonate structured sheets are available in several thicknesses from four to 16mm. Normally seven to eight millimeters is used for hobby greenhouses. To insure long weatherability and durability purchase a co-extruded or coated polycarbonate sheet. These sheets will yellow less than an untreated material. Polycarbonates also have less flammability and higher impact resistance to hail or vandalism than the acrylic materials. For example, a six millimeter sheet will take a blow from a 10 pound steel ball dropped seven feet without cracking.

Acrylic structured sheets are available in eight and 16 millimeters thick sheets. Although they've been in use in the U.S. for only 10 years, a similar single-skin material — plexiglas — has been around much longer. This material does not yellow with age. Plexiglas is used in place of curved pane glass and in areas that might be subject to breakage.

Improvements in film plastics are still coming out of manufacturers research centers. Increases in strength, clarity, life and energy conservation are recent developments. Because most films do not have as long a life as rigid glazings, they are not used as frequently for hobby greenhouses.

The stronger co-polymer plastics called "greenhouse plastics" will give good service for two to three years. These can be purchased with an infrared radiation inhibitor that reduces the heat loss from inside the greenhouse by up to 20 percent on a clear night. Monsanto calls theirs "Cloud 9" and FVG America has named theirs "Sunsaver." Although the light transmission is the same as other greenhouse grade plastic films, the cloudy appearance diffuses the light.

Window Greenhouse

A window greenhouse is a good choice where you have limited space and time for gardening. A south facing window is best but windows facing east or west can also be used.

The window to which your greenhouse is attached must be the double hung casement type (opening up and down) or one that slides sideways because the plants must be accessible from the inside. Because the window greenhouse contains such a small volume of air, more attention to heating and cooling needs is required.

All types of greenhouses can give many hours of relaxation and enjoyment. The most common complaint is that it gets too small too quickly.

WINDOW GREENHOUSES

Linda Yang

A partment gardeners go to great lengths to keep their house-plants happy. This includes altering their homes to suit their plants. One major modification is a window greenhouse, which can also be an attractive extension to a room.

The idea for the first commercially produced window greenhouse is believed to have originated about 25 years ago when Cyrus D'Amato was preparing to display patio doors at the New York Flower Show. To make his glass products more appealing, he carved an opening in the wall of the display trailer and filled it with a "glass box" of plants.

He noticed that the visitors to the show were more intrigued with the box bursting with blooms than the storm doors he was trying to sell them. And so, the window greenhouse was born.

Mr. D'Amato's design was the inspiration for Lord & Burnham's Jiffy Window Greenhouse which has sold well over the years and has recently been revised to feature double insulated glass. The 17-inch-deep units are constructed of

aluminum and can be purchased in varying widths (36" to 72") and heights (36" to 72"). With the option obtaining additional shelves for the units, Lord & Burnham advertises that their window greenhouses provide plenty of room to grow.

It was to Lord & Burnham that Kurt Munkacsi turned when his dozens of cactus plants overgrew his windows. A New York City based recording engineer and record producer, Mr. Munkacsi's involvement with houseplants began innocently enough when a friend gave him a tiny *Lithops*. Fascinated by that succulent, he continued to buy them by the score. The growing space dwindled in the downtown loft that is his home and office and a window greenhouse seemed the way to grow. His succulent collection is now comfortably accommodated in an arid window greenhouse.

Pat Beadle, a production manager with a film company, bought her unit to provide a humid atmosphere for her scores of orchids, begonias and ferns. Her husband assumed that the greenhouse would ensure that her bulging collection would be confined to one place. But Mrs. Beadle has used her unit to propagate even more plants, distributing them to other sills. Her husband,

LINDA YANG, *New York, NY writes about gardening for the* **Home Section** *of* **The New York Times**. *She is author of* **The Terrace Gardener's Handbook** *and* **The City Gardener's Handbook**.

accepting the inevitable, devised mesh screen doors that separate the greenhouse unit from the room and keep their cats from jumping into propagating trays.

Although these two city gardeners employ their window greenhouses to provide completely different climates, the unit they use is basically the same. And they both faced similar installation problems. The installation charges are usually extra, but while it's not impossible to "do it yourself," it's not so easy in the city. Lord & Burnham suggests that a local contractor be used to help follow the instructions provided.

Projecting window greenhouse units are usually not a problem on city walls that are set back from the building line. But, if the unit is planned for an area where it will overhang the street, building department safety procedures must be followed. So it is best to check with your local authorities before you begin.

A typical installation for masonry buildings entails first fastening a wood frame to the outside walls with expansion shields and lag bolts. The greenhouse is then attached to this frame, completely surrounding the existing window, from which the sashes may then be removed.

For penthouse or brownstone residents, this may mean using a long ladder or scaffolding, or a cable from the roof to temporarily suspend the unit while it is being secured.

Mr. Munkacsi's situation was particularly challenging and his solution was logical and innovative. Since his loft is on a high floor and his window area is not accessible on the exterior from either below or above, he used a custom-sized unit that would fit through his window from inside the room. Friends in the stage construction industry fabricated a heavy aluminum frame that he used to replace the original wood window sashes. Working from indoors, he could then slide the greenhouse through the window opening and attach its sides directly to the inner faces of this new aluminum frame.

Both Mrs. Beadle and Mr. Munkacsi removed the original windows so their greenhouses open into the room and benefit from apartment heat. His houseplants require a dry environment, hers need humidity. Their window greenhouses have made it pleasurable for them to do just that. ❦

PORTIONS OF THIS ARTICLE FIRST APPEARED IN THE HOME SECTION OF THE NEW YORK TIMES.

11

GARDEN ROOMS FOR EVERYONE

OGDEN TANNER

Garden rooms are designed primarily for people, with an accent on comfort, outdoor views and the sun. PHOTOS BY GEORGE TALOUMIS

n recent years glass additions have become increasingly popular, not only as greenhouses for serious indoor gardening, but as rooms to live in, eat in, take baths in and almost everything else. In the pages of magazines, happy families are pictured using theirs in all sorts of mouth-watering ways: sunbathing in the dead of winter, breakfasting among potted palms, splashing merrily in hot tubs with wine glasses raised high, entertaining dinner guests by candlelight under a sky spangled with stars.

Call them sun rooms, solariums, garden rooms or whatever you like, these spaces differ from working greenhouses in one major respect: they are designed primarily for people, with the accent on comfort, outdoor views and the sun itself. While some decorative plants are usually part of the scene, they are sup-

OGDEN TANNER *is a former editor of the* **Time-Life Encyclopedia of Gardening** *and the author of* **Garden Rooms**.

porting players, not the stars. Fortunately, there are many species whose basic needs for light, temperature and humidity do not conflict with those of human occupants.

Among other attractions, a prefabricated glass unit can be less expensive than a conventionally built addition, and can add at least its cost to the resale value of a house. Moreover, if properly designed, it can trap, store and distribute sun heat, sharing its warmth with the rest of a home and reducing household heating bills.

The ideal exposure for a garden room, like a greenhouse, is south for maximum winter sun. Southeast will provide welcome morning sunlight, and is a good choice for a breakfast room; a southwest exposure yields more afternoon sun and may provide a nice view of sunsets, but will require shading, especially in summer, against hot afternoon rays. Unlike a working greenhouse, a live-in glass addition can even be placed

An enclosed breezeway using lots of glass becomes a garden room.

on the north side, though it will receive mostly indirect light and no solar heating, and will have to be furnished with plants that tolerate lower light.

The most practical shape for the average sun room is a rectangle with its length along the side of the house measuring about one and-a-half to two times its projecting width—the greater the glass area facing south the more sun it will get, and the greater the wall area the sun room shares with the house, the greater the potential for an exchange of solar heat between the two.

Manufacturers' units, which are generally cheaper than custom-built designs, come in a variety of choices, from a glorified bay window three-feet deep and eight-feet long, which can serve as a modest enlargement of an existing room, to a two-story solarium 20-feet deep and more than 50-feet long—big enough for an indoor swimming pool. A common tendency among budget-conscious homeowners is to order the smallest size they think suitable to their purposes, only to discover that the new space is used so much it doesn't seem big enough. Because of square-foot economies inherent in construction, installing a larger model can actually yield as much as 50 percent more space at only 25 percent more cost.

Units with wooden structural frames provide a substantial, natural-looking extension of a house, and can be stained or painted any color. Most manufacturers' models, however, are made of slimmer aluminum members, generally with dark bronze or white baked-enamel finishes that are virtually maintenance-free. The best units have secure seals against air and water leaks, thermal "breaks" to minimize conduction of heat (and cold) through the metal, and gutters to carry off condensation on the inside of the glass.

Rigid plastics can be used, particularly on roof sections and end walls, but for maximum light and views most sun rooms are enclosed in ordinary glass, which is highly transparent, scratchproof and durable. The annealed glass used today is strong enough to resist breakage under normal conditions, though many manufacturers recommend tempered or laminated glass, particularly for high-use areas and overhead glazing.

Double, and even triple, insulating glass is also available, and should be considered in northern areas to prevent heat loss on cold winter nights. A further option is glass treated with low-emissivity or "low-e" coating, which admits light and solar heat, then traps the heat by reflecting reradiation from objects inside. Besides being energy efficient, low-e glass can reduce condensation, block much of the ultraviolet light that fades indoor fabrics, and make the inside glass warmer to the touch.

One problem with a year-round, live-in glass addition is that it may get not too little sun but too much. Provisions should be made to shade the room in summer, by well-placed deciduous trees and/or by screening devices like roll-down blinds, which are sold by most manufacturers. (Some offer units with motorized blinds that run on tracks, or narrow, adjustable louvers that are actually sandwiched between two layers of insulating glass.) Bronze-tinted reflecting glass, which cuts light and heat transmission drastically, may be a desirable option in locations where there is excessive heat or glare, though it may limit plant growth and the color quality of the light inside does not appeal to everyone.

To provide permanent shade, and more efficient insulation against winter cold, some solarium units eliminate overhead glass entirely by using a solid, sloping roof with an overhang, or reduce the amount of glass by piercing a solid roof with individual skylights. A well-

14

designed space of this kind blocks high summer sun but allows low winter rays to penetrate and warm the room, and is often used in energy-efficient solar designs (described below).

In addition to shading, adequate ventilation is vital for both people and plants. If possible, doors and windows should be placed to capture cross-drafts from prevailing summer breezes; this natural flow can be aided by an exhaust fan high on one end wall, with pivoting intake louvers on the opposite wall. Adjustable vents along the roof line, either hand-operated or automatic, may also be desirable to release a buildup of heat at the top of the room. A slowly rotating ceiling fan will provide a gentle, constant movement of air, mixing layers of different temperatures, and in winter bringing warm air down from above.

The flooring in any sun room that gets constant use should be durable, moisture-proof and easy to keep clean, especially if plants are set on the floor where dampness can accumulate under their pots (and can soon ruin carpets or wood). Vinyl flooring is available in many patterns, and is both resilient and economical; flagstone or brick set in mortar gives an attractive "terrace" look. An especially handsome material is ceramic tile, which comes in a range of warm browns, yellows and reds. While glazed tile looks nice and shiny it can be slippery when damp; unglazed tiles have greater skid resistance.

To get still more out of a sun room, consider giving it some features of so-called "passive solar" design. Almost any glass addition will add warmth to a house when exposed to the sun, but it may lose that warmth and more, unless it can be closed off from the rest of the house on cold nights or cloudy winter days. The simplest way to avoid this is to leave the old exterior house wall intact, open existing windows and doors to bring heat from the sun room into the rest of the house when the sun is shining, and close them when the temperature of the sun room drops.

For greater efficiency, some owners install closable vents high on the old exterior wall to allow accumulated warm air to flow into the house, and more vents near the floor to allow cool air to flow from the house to the outer space, thus setting up a natural convection cycle. (A thermostatically controlled fan in an upper vent can speed the process; if it is reversible, it can also be used to force warm air into the sun room to keep the temperature up on cool nights.)

Much the same effect can be obtained by replacing smaller doors and windows in the old wall with tall sliding-glass doors. When these doors are slid back by day, warm air flows into the house through the upper part of the opening, and cool air flows out from the house into the sun room along the floor. When the doors are closed at night, their double glazing provides insulation from the lower temperatures of the outer space, which can be allowed to go as low as 45 degrees or 50 degrees Fahrenheit without harm to most plants (many species, indeed, prefer cooler conditions at night). As a bonus, sliding doors can also brighten dark living areas and make the sun room a more visible, and appealing, part of the house.

To store sun heat by day, and slowly release it at night to keep temperatures from going too low, a sun room should have some materials with "thermal mass." The most common is masonry, in the form of a floor of ceramic tile or brick laid on a concrete slab, or interior walls of brick, concrete block or stone.

For more specific advice on adapting such a room to your particular situation and requirements, consult architects and greenhouse manufacturers who specialize in solar design. 🍂

The author's conservatory has a glass roof supported by a cast metal framework.
The stone walls match the house.

THE CONSERVATORY

J. LIDDON PENNOCK

M r. Webster defines "conservatory" as a dwelling-attached glass house for growing plants, especially ornamental cultivated plants. He infers, and correctly so, that this type of structure is created to be a showcase for decorative plants rather than a growing greenhouse.

A conservatory should not be equipped with benches which are necessary to bring plants from the seedling or rooted cutting stage to total fruition. Instead, it should feature display areas to give the impression of planted beds. A conservatory is designed to have the feel-

J. LIDDON PENNOCK, *Jr. of Meadowbrook, PA has served as honorary president for the National Herb Society, president of the Philadelphia Horticultural Society, and chairman for the Philadelphia Flower Show and President of the Academy of Music. He was the horticultural designer, decorator-designate for the White House during the Nixon administration.*

ing of an outdoor garden transported inside.

Although it may seem like a simple feat, it is not easy to preserve the illusion of floral bounty and, at the same time, heat a decorative plant room. The obvious place for radiation units would be in front of, or directly under the windows. This area, of course, is also the ideal location for the massing of plants. Radiant heat under the floor surface is another possible solution that proves unsuitable because specimen plants placed directly on the floor are important to the appearance of the design and yet they suffer just as any plant would suffer if placed on a warm stove.

The best location for heating units is directly under the entry or exit doors where plants would obviously never be located. Oil-fueled units are the most cost-effective system for heating a conservatory. They can be housed under the floor surface and covered with a heavy grill the length of the door openings. These units come equipped with remarkably silent fans that will efficiently circulate air throughout the room, thus insuring an even temperature at both the ceiling and the floor level. The temperature can be regulated by a thermostat to control the variation in temperature, day or night. Hot water is piped to each unit and connected directly to the hot water system emanating from the same furnaces that heat the residence.

In Meadowbrook Farm's glass room conservatory, the high roof ceiling of the room is composed of one-half-inch-thick plate glass, supported by a cast metal structural framework which rests on stone walls that match the house itself. As an alternative, an A-line roof could have been used, consisting of a strong center joist and supporting rafters about 18 inches apart with glazed thermo-pane and a double walled clear plastic material called Lexan or Polygal (a General Elec-

tric product). The interior surfaces are simply cement stucco, mixed without lime due to the high moisture content of the atmosphere.

The walls give the structure the look of a glass room rather than a working greenhouse. The room also has openings in the walls equipped with sliding panels and screening. The heating units are located under these two doorways.

Indirect lighting fixtures were installed in the ceilings of each of the recessed doors and windows. The valences are simulated carved wood panels created out of white styrofoam and molded to look like antique paneling. They conceal the sources of all the interior lighting. Additional illumination through the glass roof is supplied by 150 watt flood lights affixed outdoors to the upper eaves above the glass room, contributing considerable drama to the night lighting effect.

Ficus pumila, the climbing fig, was used to conceal the metal rafters. At the base of each narrow wall area there is a 12 by 14-inch excavation cut through the marble floor into the base soil. Small ficus plants were then inserted in the exterior walls of the residence. As the vine grew up the interior wall, one leader was encouraged while most laterals were removed. The vines finally reached the rafters and commenced to cover the metal framework eventually developing into hanging swags and other forms. These have now taken the place of many hanging baskets which were used to grace the originally bare looking structural ceiling.

The eight narrow trenches containing the ficus are the only permanent planting beds. All other plants are displayed in movable galvanized metal trays matching the width and length of all the glass wall areas, except the doorways. This enables the pattern of the plant placement areas to be changed depending on the season and the quantities of plant material available. The trays are filled with pebbles to the depth of several inches, so that if there is an overflow of water, the pots will rest above the water level. This is an important drainage factor that prevents the plants from having wet feet and thus root rot. The dampness in the pots and trays provide sufficient moisture throughout the room.

Suitable furniture is of prime importance. Furniture made of wood, aluminum, iron or wicker with upholstery that can withstand the moisture of the room is suitable. Sculpture or other ornamental features adds to the decorative effect.

In summer, the conservatory is shaded by trees—pines and *Magnolia grandiflora*, planted on the west and south sides of the structure. If deciduous trees were used they would produce shade when in leaf and good light when the leaves have fallen. If tree plantings are not feasible, provide shade with the adjustable slat screens, saran netting, or a whitewash compound to coat the conservatory roof.

The maintenance of a conservatory could be compared to that involved in any flower garden, where, to maintain perfection, a back-up area of plants is grown and dug to fill in the gaps that occur during the season. Ideally, a small working greenhouse provides the replacement material.

If orchids are part of the scenery, remove them when they are not in flower. The blooms have an exceedingly long life-span which make orchids an absolute must for this type of setting. Despite their aura of glamour, orchid plants are relatively simple to grow.

Seasonal plants such as forced azaleas and chrysanthemums can be used in a conservatory. But they must be removed when not in flower. Flowering plants that bloom over a prolonged period should be incorporated wherever possible. Foliage plants are an equally important element because they provide a leafy background.

Most importantly, creating and maintaining a conservatory is an extremely rewarding horticultural and aesthetic experience. 🍎

White wicker furniture and white latticework are interesting textural elements in this garden room filled with flowering plants.

GUIDELINES FOR BUILDING A GREENHOUSE

LINDA YANG

I n 1987 more than 10,000 hobbyists' greenhouses were built in the U. S., according to Dr. Harold E. Gray, the executive director of the National Greenhouse Manufacturers' Association. The average cost of an 8-by-15-foot structure was $2,000 to $3,000; to make it a working greenhouse that figure must be multiplied two and a half times. "Less than a second car," Dr. Gray commented.

There are more than 100 greenhouse manufacturers nationwide, offering a wide variety of styles. The association has prepared a list of them, as well as guidelines on lighting, ventilation, siting and other considerations. These are available free from the association. Send a self-addressed, stamped envelope to P.O. Box 567, Pana, IL 62557.

A magazine, *Greenhouses for Living*, is devoted to the subject, with articles on questions like how to select a builder, and how to finance it. Issues cost $6.95 in bookstores and $8.00, postpaid, from 350 Fifth Avenue, Suite 6124, New York, NY 10001.

Every city has special code requirements concerning greenhouses. In New York, building permits are required, and people living in cooperatives must have permission from the building's board. Laminated safety glass or wire glass that will not shatter is mandatory. An architect or engineer is usually consulted for roof-top construction because of code requirements regarding snow load and wind shear.

THIS ARTICLE FIRST APPEARED IN THE HOME SECTION OF THE NEW YORK TIMES, THURSDAY, JANUARY 21, 1988.

Check your local building codes before starting plans for your greenhouse.

SOLAR GREENHOUSES

COLLEEN ARMSTRONG

Generally speaking, all greenhouses are solar greenhouses because heat from the sunlight is trapped in the glazed structure. While energy-efficient solar greenhouses maximize the amount of solar gain (the primary source for heat) and minimize heat loss during the heating season, an equal emphasis is placed on climate control. These greenhouses can vary from being 100% passive solar without back-up heat, or a combination of solar and supplemental heat.

When planning a solar greenhouse, select a design that suits your needs. There are many designs for solar greenhouses. Some people build solar structures to function as a solarium or a space heater for the home. You can choose between a custom greenhouse or a kit (see table—Solar Greenhouse Kits). Custom greenhouses tend to be more expensive buildings because they are designed to blend with the existing house. One advantage to kit greenhouses is the opportunity to visit a model or an owner in your area. Ask the greenhouse owners what is satisfactory and less than satisfactory about the kit. A financial plan is equally important; solar greenhouses are more expensive than the conventional types. Solar heat is not necessarily free! A low cost, do-it-yourself

COLLEEN ARMSTRONG, E. Falmouth, MA is a research associate at the New Alchemy Institute in E. Falmouth, MA which specializes in alternative energy systems.

solar greenhouse starts at $15 per square foot; an aesthetically pleasing, quality greenhouse averages at $100 per square foot. Also, check with your local building inspector for the code laws in your town. It may save costly delays in the future.

Site considerations depend upon your choice of greenhouse—freestanding or attached. Locate freestanding greenhouses where there is plenty of light and few obstructions from trees or other buildings. There may be a warm pocket on your property where the greenhouse could be nestled away from northern winds. In cold climates, freestanding greenhouses require more thermal mass for heat storage than do attached greenhouses.

Attached solar greenhouses are usually built onto the southern side of a house where at least six hours of sunlight reaches the area. These greenhouses have the advantage of exhausting excess heat into the house, and receiving heat from the house at night. Also, the common wall between house and greenhouse protects it from harsh, cold winds. At the same time, it restricts light from entering the northern section of the greenhouse and consequently, attached greenhouses are less productive than freestanding solar greenhouses.

A site survey to determine the most suitable location for an attached solar greenhouse should include the best possible southern orientation, the least shading by trees or other obstructions, designated lot lines and prevailing winter winds. True south is different from "south" on the compass; solar greenhouse textbooks discuss the adjustments needed for your area. A greenhouse facing true south gains the most light from the winter sun. If this direction isn't possible, locate the greenhouse 20 to 30 degrees east or west of south. Spend some time in the winter months plotting the sun's path over your desired location. Sketch out where the shadows lie and note the angle of the sun. Within range of due south, the winter sunlight should be perpendicular to the tilted glazing. Reference books will give you the sun path chart for your latitude (see Further Reading). Equally important, you want to plot the altitude and azimuth angles of any obstructions to the sun.

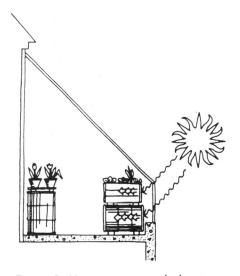

FIGURE 1. Heat storage and planting beds placed behind the glazing will be heated by the sun. The warm root zone will boost winter plant growth.

Other site considerations should include the average weather patterns for your area. Predominantly cloudy days in the winter season will dramatically reduce solar radiation when it is most needed. Note if your desired location has any peculiar microclimate qualities such as wind protection or fog. Evaluate the terrain for your greenhouse site; check for proper drainage. All of this information will aid you in deciding whether your site is suitable for a solar design.

Not all greenhouses can operate on solar energy alone. The slope of the glazing should maximize the amount of solar

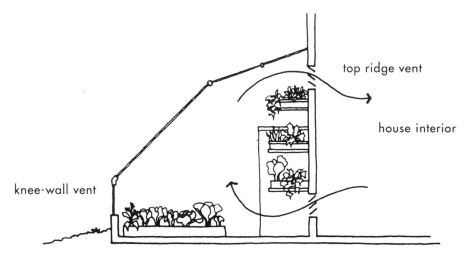

FIGURE 2. Daytime air circulation in an attached greenhouse.

radiation in the winter months. To determine the slope of the southern roof glazing for your area, simply add 10 to 20 degrees to your latitude or refer to radiation tables for the best glazing angle (see Further Reading). In order to enhance solar radiation passing into the greenhouse, consider glazing the end walls and selecting framing materials which will minimize shading. Light is important for both passive solar heating and photosynthesis. Even though a larger glazed area has more heat loss, sufficient heat storage can justify it. Your choice of glazing materials and their longevity will also affect the light transmission into the greenhouse. Reflected light can also be a source of solar energy. White paint on the interior northern wall can reflect the incoming light back onto the growing area. Materials surrounding the greenhouse, such as snow, white sand or gravel can reflect light.

During the heating season, reducing heat loss is important. Heat loss can occur by radiation, conduction or convection. In a greenhouse, most of the heat is lost from conduction through the roof, walls and air leakage out of cracks and crevices. Double glazing can effectively reduce heat loss without sacrificing light quality. The air pocket in between the two glazings limits heat loss through conduction and convection. Insulating the foundation and north wall buffers the building from cold winds and frozen soils. Caulking around overlapping pieces of glazing reduces air leakage. Movable insulation which covers the glazed roof or growing area acts as a thermal blanket. Several kit greenhouses offer accessories such as thermal curtains or shades. The Chinese use rice mats to cover their earthen bermed greenhouses. Other materials such as rigid foam insulation, reflective films and fabrics, and bubble plastics are suitable for night insulation. Thermal curtains or panels can be designed to cover the outer or inner glazing surfaces.

Solar greenhouses reduce the outflow of heat by storing it in some type of thermal mass. Heat is stored most efficiently in water, and to a lesser degree in mud, masonry, rock and earth. Water can be stored in one-gallon containers stacked on top of one another, fifty-five gallon drums, tanks constructed from plastic reinforced with fiberglass or various sized containers. A general rule of thumb for cold climates: for every square foot of glazed area, one-half a cubic foot of water is recommended for heat storage. Usually water tanks are placed against the north wall where the water can absorb the heat during the day and radi-

FIGURE 3. Sucessional Planting Scheme for Vegetables in Solar Greenhouses.

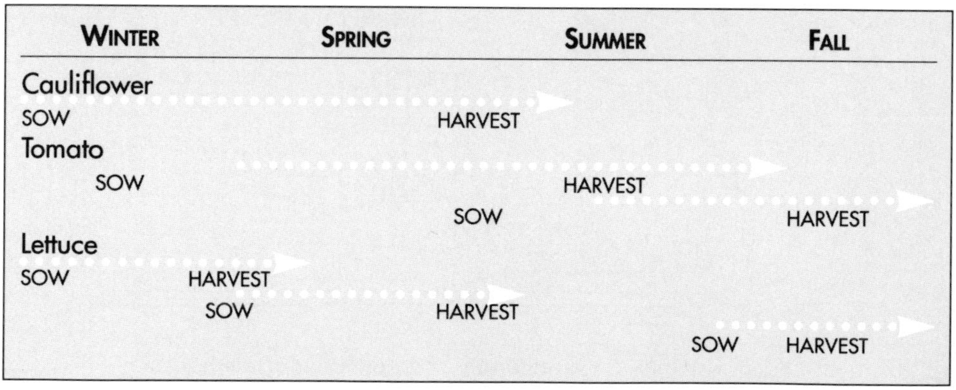

	WINTER	SPRING	SUMMER	FALL
Cauliflower				
	SOW	HARVEST		
Tomato				
	SOW		HARVEST	
		SOW		HARVEST
Lettuce				
	SOW	HARVEST		
		SOW	HARVEST	
			SOW	HARVEST

ate heat at night. Paint the water storage containers a dark color to increase heat absorption.

In small greenhouses, water may be an impractical thermal mass. Even though masonry has less than half the heat capacity of water, it has some advantages. A concrete wall can double as both

VEGETABLE VARIETIES FOR SOLAR GREENHOUSES

VEGETABLE	NAME OF VARIETY	LIGHT CONDITION
Cool Season		
Beet	Ruby Queen	Direct
Cauliflower	Opaal	Direct
Celery	Utah 52-70 Improved	Direct
Chard, Swiss and Red	Fordhook, Rhubarb	Partial
Chinese Cabbage	Yellow Radish Bud	Direct
Endive	Full-Heart Batavian	Direct, Partial
	Green Curled	Direct, Partial
Kale	Gr. Curled Dwarf Scotch	Direct, Partial
Lettuce, loose-leaf	Green Ice	Direct
Lettuce, buttercrunch	Salina, Vasco	Direct
Lettuce, romaine	Winter Density	Direct
Pac Choi	Pac Choi	Direct, Partial
Radicchio		Direct
Warm Season		
Cucumber	Lemon	Direct
European Cucumber	Coronna, Vetomil, Super Sandra	
Melons	Ambrosia, Charentais Improved	Direct
Peppers, Green	Ace, California Wonder	Direct
Peppers, Red	Sweet Round Red	
Peppers, Yellow		
Tomato	Sweet 100 (Cherry) Caruso Park's VFNT greenhouse Jumbo Floramerica Vendor	Direct

thermal mass and structural element for both house and greenhouse and it requires less maintenance than water. Thick masonry walls (six to eight inches) tend to be more expensive than water storage systems. Deep soil growing beds absorb the heat from the sun, yet they are an inefficient thermal mass. A practical and old technique for heat storage is to build the greenhouse into a hillside and use the surrounding soil as insulation. "Pit greenhouses" are a variation on this theme; they are built into the ground and approximately two-thirds of the greenhouse is insulated by the ground. These greenhouses are limited for light but simply designed. An expensive and sophisticated alternative is to move the hot air from the top of the greenhouse into a rock storage area below the greenhouse floor. Heat from the warmed rocks is conducted into the soil beds and surrounds the plants. These systems require electrical energy for fans and ductwork.

Climate control is an essential design component. In an effort to store the daytime heat, solar greenhouses have less regulated temperature regimes than their conventional counterparts. In most 100% passive solar greenhouses, a wide diurnal temperature fluctuation occurs throughout the heating season. Daytime temperatures can rise to 70 to 80 degrees F while nighttime temperatures can drop from 50 to 40 degrees F. Some plants will not tolerate such wide fluctuations. If optimum climate conditions are necessary, then you should design for both passive solar heat and supplemental heat.

Poorly designed solar greenhouses have problems with overheating. Hot air can be ventilated from the greenhouse either passively or mechanically. Passive or natural ventilation is based on air movement by convection; warm air is exhausted out of the greenhouse while cool fresh air is drawn in. The most com-mon natural ventilation design has windows or vents at the top of the greenhouse and low vents near the floor. The total vent area for natural ventilation should be one-sixth of the floor area with upper vents 20 to 30 percent larger than the lower vents. For windy areas, doors placed on the windward and leeward sides of the greenhouse provide adequate cross ventilation. For windless summer days, natural ventilation can be encouraged by designing for the stack effect; solar chimneys are such devices that take advantage of buoyant warm air escaping out of tall, narrow chimneylike boxes with glazing on one side. All vents should be sealed to prevent heat loss in the winter. For absent greenhouse operators, automatic ventilation is compulsory.

Mechanical ventilation is more consistent and reliable than passive methods. Usually, a wall-mounted exhaust fan combined with side vents at the opposite side of the greenhouse is sufficient. Energy-conserving solar greenhouses have ventilation rates of four to 10 air exchanges per hour. Most commercial greenhouses recommend two to four times this rate. When selecting your fan, let this general rule of thumb be your guide: fan capacity should handle 200 cubic feet per minute for every 1,000 cubic feet of greenhouse volume. Attached greenhouses should have two sets of vents; one set for exchange into the house during fall, winter and spring seasons and another for ventilating hot air to the outside throughout the summer months.

Shading the greenhouse is another technique for controlling temperature. Most glazings can be sprayed with a shading compound which is non-toxic and easily removed with soap and water. Other options are shade cloths which are available in various grades and covering the greenhouse glazing with vegetative vines such as cucumbers, melons or run-

- Passive solar heat gain & distribution   • Passive summer ventilation
- Deep soil growing beds   • Benches & shelves for flats & plants
- Water tubes for heat storage

nerbeans. Shading may be removed earlier than conventional greenhouse shading to access passive solar heating in the fall.

Solar greenhouses can be used for season extension or year-round gardening. In northern climates, greenhouse temperature conditions mimic two seasons, spring and summer. The greenhouse glazing acts as membrane to the outdoors and the interior temperatures are sensitive to the change of seasons. Careful plant selection can make the difference between success and failure. Many growers concentrate on vegetable production in solar greenhouses because many cool-weather crops such as lettuce, cauliflower, Oriental greens, and scallions prefer springlike temperatures during the winter months. Table lists vegetable varieties best suited for solar greenhouses in northern climates. Southern growers have more flexibility with their winter selection; however, plants that respond to long day length should be avoided during short day length periods.

Many solar greenhouse growers will start their cool weather seedlings in late summer in order to have mature, ready-to-harvest vegetables before the gray days of winter begin. For a steady harvest of leafy greens, pick the outside leaves instead of cutting the entire plant. The mature plant will continue to grow and produce throughout the coldest months of the year. Parsley, coriander, dill, and chives are tasty additions to the list of winter greens. Flowering plants that prefer cool temperatures and thrive in solar greenhouses include viola, calendula, primula, alstroemeria, freesia, nasturtium, alyssum, sweet pea, snapdragons and stock. Many orchids such as cymbidium, dendrobium, odontoglossum, cypripedium and miltonia flourish in the cool, moist climate.

Solar greenhouses have an extended summer season; heat-loving vegetables and flowers can be grown for six months or longer. Early season tomatoes, European cucumbers (the long, seedless, burpless variety), peppers and eggplant can be harvested for twelve to twenty weeks. Annual flowers such as marigold, dwarf dahlia, morning glory, impatiens, begonia and salvia can be sown in early winter; soon thereafter they'll offer splashes of color.

Developing a plan for successional planting makes for steady production as well. Figure 3 is one example of an annual planting guide. As years go by, you will learn the individual characteristics of your greenhouse and you can modify the planting scheme. ❧

FURTHER READING

Craft, M.A. Ed. *Winter Greens.* Renewable Energy in Canada. Firefly Books Ltd., Scarborough, Ontario, Canada, 1983.

Hirshberg, Gary and Tracy Calvan, Eds. "Solar Greenhouse Gardening," pp 49-88, *Gardening For All Seasons.* New Alchemy Institute. Brick House Pub., Andover, MA, 1983.

Mazria, Edward. *The Passive Solar Energy Book.* Rodale Press, Emmaus, PA, 1980.

Shapiro, A.M. *The Homeowner's Complete Handbook for Add-On Solar Greenhouses & Sunspaces.* Rodale Press, Emmaus, PA, 1985.

Smith, Shane. *The Bountiful Solar Greenhouse.* John Muir Pub., Santa Fe, NM, 1982.

Thomas, S.G. et al. *Solar Greenhouses and Sunspaces: Lessons Learned.* Prepared by the National Center for Appropriate Technology, for U.S. Department of Energy, Superintendent of Documents, U.S. Government Printing Office, Washington, D.C., DOE/CE/15095-8, 1984.

TABLE OF SOLAR GREENHOUSE KITS

ALUMINUM GREENHOUSE, INC. 14605 Lorain Ave., Cleveland, OH 44111

Charley's Greenhouse Supply, 12815 N.E. 124th St., Kirkland, WA

ENGLISH GREENHOUSE PRODUCTS CORP., 11th and Linden Sts., Camden, NJ 08102

FOUR SEASONS SOLAR PRODUCTS CORP., 910 Route 110, Farmingdale, NY 11735

HARVESTER ALL-WEATHER GREENHOUSES, 257 Main St., Chatham, NJ 07928

HORIZONS PRODUCTS, INC., 9301 E. 47th St., Kansas City, MO 64133

LORD AND BURNHAM DIVISION, Burnham Co., Box 255, Irvington, NY 10533

NATIONAL GREENHOUSE CO., P.O. Box 100, 400 E. Main St., Pana, IL 62557

NORTHERN LIGHT GREENHOUSE, GARDENERS SUPPLY CO., 128 Intervale Rd., Burlington, VT 05401

J.A. NEARING CO., INC., 9390 Davis Ave., Laurel, MD 20707

PACIFIC COAST GREENHOUSE MANUFACTURING CO., 8360 Industrial Ave., Cotati, CA 94928

SOLAR RESOURCES, INC., P.O. Box 1848, Taos, NM 87571

VEGETABLE FACTORY, INC., Sunbeam Structures Division, 71 Vanderbilt Ave., New York, NY 10169

CONTROLLING THE ENVIRONMENT IN A GREENHOUSE

John W. Bartok, Jr.

Controlling the environment within a greenhouse in both winter and summer is important to the production of quality plants. Heat, light, humidity and air quality are all crucial factors. There is a large selection of equipment available that will fit almost any greenhouse.

Heat

If the greenhouse is to be sufficiently warm to stimulate good plant growth

A profusion of plants creates a rainbow of colors in one of Logee's greenhouses in Danielson, Connecticut.

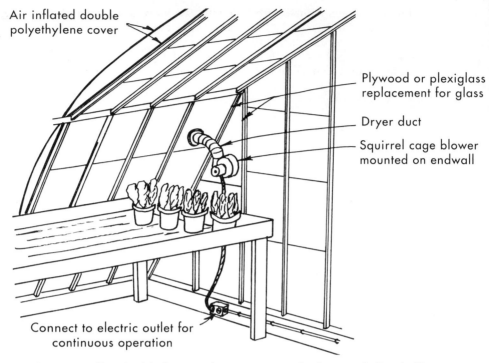

Air inflated double polyethylene cover

Plywood or plexiglass replacement for glass

Dryer duct

Squirrel cage blower mounted on endwall

Connect to electric outlet for continuous operation

Install a double-layer poly cover to cut the heating bill in half.

during the winter, a heating system is needed. If your greenhouse is attached to your home, it may be possible to connect it with the home heating system. The first step is to determine whether the system has the extra capacity needed to provide greenhouse heat. Check with a heating contractor. For hot water systems, a separate zone should be installed including a thermostat located in the greenhouse. For hot air systems, a separate control circuit and motorized damper are needed.

Where the central heating system is not large enough, or the greenhouse is free standing, an independent heater can be used. The electric heater is convenient, clean, efficient and easy to install; but electric energy is more expensive than other fuels. The heater should have a built-in thermostat and circulation fan. Also bear in mind that adequate electric supply and wiring is required.

Space heaters are commonly used to heat hobby greenhouses. Self-contained units that burn natural gas, LP gas or fuel oil and distribute the air with a blower are best. A separate thermostat located at plant level gives good temperature control. Some of the products of combustion are toxic to both humans and plants, therefore fuel-burning heaters must always be vented to the outside. Non-vented heaters should never be used in a greenhouse. With all heating systems, even distribution of heat and good temperature control are necessary to achieve uniform plant growth.

The amount of heat required depends on the temperature difference between inside and outside, the amount of greenhouse surface area and glazing, as well as the tightness of the construction. As a rule of thumb, for a free-standing greenhouse located in a northern climate with 100 sq. ft. floor area, it will take 25,000 Btu/hr heat capacity to maintain 60 degrees F inside on a night when it is 0 degrees F outside. If the greenhouse has double glazing, this can be reduced by one third. For an attached greenhouse or a greenhouse located in a southern climate, only 12,000 Btu/hr will be required.

There are several methods for reducing heat loss and thereby decreasing heating costs. One of the simplest and most effective is to line the inside of the greenhouse with plastic film over the winter months. Clear polyethylene, six mil. thick is easily installed and can be reused for several years. It is available from greenhouse suppliers and lumber yards. One disadvantage is that it will reduce the amount of light inside the greenhouse by 10 to 15 percent. In addition, if your greenhouse is equipped with ridge vents, it is difficult to find a method for opening the plastic to let heat escape on sunny winter days.

If your greenhouse has a lot of hanging baskets or obstructions overhead, it may not be practical to use the inside liner. Instead, many growers place a double-inflated poly cover over their greenhouses for the winter. The two layers are separated by the slight air pressure from a squirrel cage blower, about the size used in a hair dryer. The blower operates continuously to keep the two layers separated.

The double-inflated poly cover is easily installed. Two sheets of greenhouse-grade plastic, large enough to cover the roof and sidewalls, are needed. The plastic can be attached by

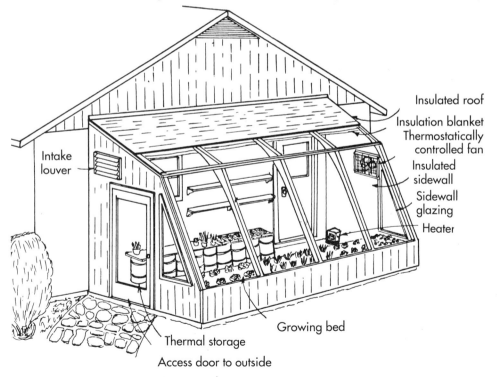

Insulated roof
Insulation blanket
Thermostatically controlled fan
Insulated sidewall
Sidewall glazing
Heater
Intake louver
Growing bed
Thermal storage
Access door to outside

Attached solar greenhouse for growing plants

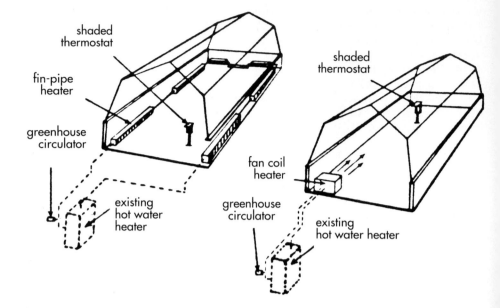

shaded thermostat

fin-pipe heater

greenhouse circulator

existing hot water heater

shaded thermostat

fan coil heater

greenhouse circulator

existing hot water heater

using either wood furring strips or one of the aluminum extrusions available from greenhouse suppliers. The following procedures may be used:

● Wash the outside glass to ensure better light transmission.

● Cover or remove all sharp edges that could puncture the plastic. Duct tape and foam padding work well.

● Attach the plastic securing devices to the foundation wall and sidewalls. If vents are to remain operational, attach the securing devices just below the vent. Use through bolts or long screws.

● Remove a section of glass where the duct connection will be made to the inner layer of plastic.

● Select a calm day to install the plastic.

● Fasten the plastic film with the securing devices. Pull the plastic taut but don't worry about minor wrinkles, they will disappear after inflation.

● Sidewalls can also be covered using the same procedure.

● The blower should have an output of less than 100-cubic-feet per minute and a cut-off pressure of less than 0.5-inch static pressure. These are available from greenhouse or electrical supply houses.

● Mount the blower in a location convenient to where the duct will be connected to the plastic. Flexible vacuum hose or dryer duct works well for the connection.

● Once the connection is made, the blower may be plugged into an electrical outlet and inflation started. A metal plate over the intake of the blower is used to adjust the pressure until it feels as taut as a medium-hard balloon.

● The blower should operate continuously. It will use from five to ten cents worth of electricity a day.

This method may also be used on a polyethylene-covered, wood-frame greenhouse.

Several materials are available that can be used to insulate the glass sidewalls of a greenhouse. Aircap, the polyethylene bubble material found in package cushioning, may be purchased from greenhouse suppliers. It can be attached by stapling or taping. However, insulation board is a better choice for areas where transparency is not important such as foundation walls, north walls and below benches. It is available from most lumber yards; a one or two inch thickness should be used.

When building a new greenhouse, it is wise to insulate the perimeter foundation wall to a depth of about two feet below ground level. The insulation can be placed either inside or outside.

Cooling

Greenhouses need ventilation for cooling, and to reduce high humidity and replenish carbon dioxide. Exhaust fans, in combination with inlet louvers, are a convenient method of ventilation because they can be automated by wiring them to a thermostat. If a two-speed fan is combined with this system, ventilation can begin at about half-rate when the outside air is very cold.

When installing the system, the exhaust fan should be placed on the end of the greenhouse, away from prevailing

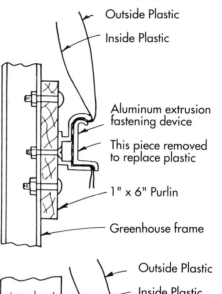

FASTENING METHODS FOR DOUBLE INFLATION GREENHOUSE COVER

Outside Plastic

Inside Plastic

Aluminum extrusion fastening device

This piece removed to replace plastic

1" x 6" Purlin

Greenhouse frame

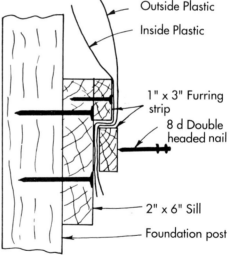

Outside Plastic

Inside Plastic

1" x 3" Furring strip

8 d Double headed nail

2" x 6" Sill

Foundation post

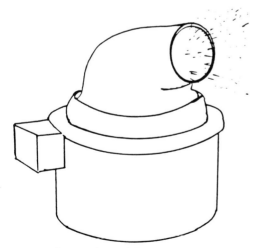

An electric humidifier will increase moisture level and cool the greenhouse.

summer winds. A motorized inlet louver at the opposite end is then controlled by the same thermostat that starts the fan. Purchase a fan that is sized so that the capacity is at least 12 cubic-feet per-minute (cfm) per square foot of floor area. This will be adequate to remove the summer heat. To overcome resistance of the fan louvers, the cfm should be measured at 0.1 inches of water pressure.

Most glass-covered greenhouses are available with vents. A continuous vent along the ridge or top of the greenhouse provides the best natural ventilation. The ridge vent operates on the principle that warm air inside the greenhouse rises to the top of the house and escapes, while cooler air enters to take its place. Side vents can help good air flow. Automatic vent controllers that open and close the ridge vent according to temperature are extremely helpful for growers who cannot constantly monitor and tend a greenhouse.

HID fixture with adjustable reflectors matches distribution with area to be lighted.

Humidity Control

Excess humidity can cause disease problems during the spring and fall months when moisture condenses on the plants. It helps to move the air with circulating fans, but a more effective means of dehumidifying a greenhouse is to replace the moist air inside with drier outside air. This is usually accomplished by cracking the vent open or turning the fan on for a few minutes.

During the hot summer days, humidity may become too low for optimal plant growth. Wetting the walks and floor area increases humidity if it is done frequently. A small humidifier can also be used.

Lighting

Light is usually the limiting factor in plant growth during the winter and on cloudy days. Two types of supplemental lighting are used.

Photoperiodic lighting for day length affects the flowering of such plants as chrysanthemums and poinsettias. Incandescent light at a very low level (less than 10 footcandles) also works well.

Supplemental lighting for photosynthesis adds to the sunlight that is needed for growth of tall foliage plants. A relatively high light level (about 500 footcandles) for several hours above the natural day length may be needed. Fluorescent lamps (usually cool white) or the newer, more efficient sodium vapor or metal halide lamps are the best choice. To control them, use a 24-hour clock timer. However, before deciding on supplemental lighting, compare the cost to the added growth of the plants. Except for high value crops such as roses, supplemental lighting has not proved to be economically worthwhile.

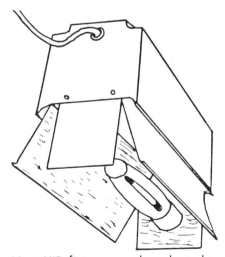

Most HID fixtures can be adapted to either metal halide or high pressure sodium lamps.

HORIZONTAL AIR FLOW

Jay S. Koths and John W. Bartok, Jr.

Plants grow better when air is continuously circulated in a greenhouse. This cools or warms the leaf surfaces and evaporates disease-promoting moisture. Also the circulation of carbon dioxide is improved, increasing growth potential. Although several systems provide air movement, the Horizontal Air Flow (HAF) method has been found to be the most effective.

The HAF concept typically uses small circulating fans operating continuously to push the air horizontally on one side of a greenhouse and back in the other direction on the other side. This creates a circular horizontal pattern. Mixing of the air occurs from the ceiling to the floor.

Other systems use different concepts. The fan-jet system uses perforated plastic tubes suspended in the peak of the greenhouse and inflated with a one-sixth to one-half horsepower fan. The lighter heated air in the upper portion of the greenhouse is forced downward through

Jay. S. Koths, *Storrs, CT is Professor Emeritus of Floriculture at the University of Connecticut.*

the holes in the tube and tries to displace the heavier, cooler air near the floor. The turbulence and plant canopy slow the air movement. Losses from friction in the tube and from forcing the air through the small diameter holes in the tube increase the motor horsepower needed and the energy used.

The turbulator system uses vertical shaft fans mounted above eave height to stir the air and force it toward the eaves and back across the floor, resulting in a cold spot below the fan. These fans draw air from a limited area and many fans may be needed.

Basic Air Movement Concept

When a fluid is enclosed in a container it may be moved in a coherent pattern with a minimum of energy. Fluid flow is energy efficient, being slowed more from turbulence caused by obstructions rather than by surface friction in the container.

This is an important concept in the movement of air (a fluid) in the greenhouse (a container). The air mass, once in motion, will continue to move until obstructions (plants and surface friction)

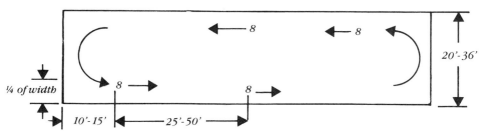

Typical HAF fan placement (16" diameter) in a narrow individual greenhouse.

35

slow it. For efficiency, the air mass should be as large and coherent as possible.

In a small greenhouse less than 25 feet long, this may be achieved by placing a fan in a corner. It is most efficient when directed down the house and located one-fourth the distance across the house and one-fourth the length of the house. In houses between 25 and 50 feet long, a second fan is placed in a similar position in the opposite corner. In a 100-foot house, four fans are placed as shown on page 35.

The fan(s) should be placed high enough so that the air stream is directed into as large a volume of air space as possible to minimize turbulence. If the greenhouse is high enough to place the bottom of the fan at least seven feet from the floor, a blade guard is not required. The top of the fan should be at least twelve inches from the roof.

If the fan has a rated, free-air delivery capacity in cubic feet per minute, this should be about three times the square feet of ground covered by the greenhouse.

For small greenhouses, the efficiency of the fan is not very important. Most small fans have shaded pole motors. A permanent split-capacitor motor will deliver perhaps 50 percent more air per unit of electricity used, and are recommended for larger installations.

Operation

The HAF fan(s) should run continuously whenever ventilation is not required. This may be done manually. If the vents are automated or exhaust fans are used, HAF may be operated with the double-throw thermostat commonly used for controlling ventilation.

After installation, introduce some smoke to observe the air movement.

Concepts

Air is heavy. A 15' x 25' x 9' high greenhouse will contain about 300 pounds of air. Once it is moving, it will coast around and little energy is required to maintain its momentum.

Installation cost is low. Air can be moved faster with less cost than with fan-jet or turbulator systems.

Uniform temperatures exist. Moving the air at 50 to 100 feet per minute will eliminate stratification of warm air in the peak of the greenhouse. This reduces heat loss and may more than pay for the fans and their operation. It also eliminates warm and cold spots.

Plants remain drier. Air passing over the leaves reduces the humid air layer and aids the control of foliar diseases.

Carbon dioxide is used more efficiently. By "scrubbing" the leaves with air, movement of carbon dioxide into the leaf is facilitated and growth enhanced.

Plants are warmer. On cool, clear nights, radiant cooling may reduce leaf temperatures to 3 degrees F below outdoor air temperatures. Leaves in greenhouses will be cooler than the air if the roof is cold. Moving air transfers heat to the leaves and warms them to near air temperature.

Plants are cooler. On sunny days solar radiation heats the plants. This may cause burn on young leaves following a prolonged period of cloudy weather. Moving air cools the plant, sometimes by more than five degrees.

Pest control may be enhanced. If smoke bombs or wettable powder dusts are used, the moving air may improve the control of insects or mites.

The concept of HAF is rapidly being adopted by commercial greenhouse operators. It may improve the environment for plant growth in hobby greenhouses. In very small greenhouses, the air may be moved in different patterns, even vertically rather than horizontally. Experiment a bit. Your plants will be happier. 🌱

In a garden room conventional blinds can provide shade.

GREENHOUSE SHADING

Harold E. Gray

Light is essential for plant growth but too much light can be harmful. High light can cause leafburn and waterloss and reduce flower color.

Many plants benefit from partial shading. Some orchids, many gesneriads,

Dr. Harold E. Gray, *Pana, IL is executive director of the National Greenhouse Manufacturers Association and director of VitroTech Corp. of Champaign, IL. He is a former professor at Cornell University.*

seedlings and foliage plants grow better when the greenhouse is shaded.

Commercial growers use a shading compound — a powder or liquid that is mixed with water and sprayed or brushed on the greenhouse surface. The degree of shading is regulated by the number of coats. The compound should be washed off in the fall using detergent.

Other shading materials include evenly spaced wood slats such as snow

Aluminum shading attached to the outside of the greenhouse can be rolled up or down by sections to achieve different rates of shading.

fence placed on the greenhouse exterior. Roll-up shades are also an option and are available from greenhouse manufacturers. These shades can be constructed of wood or aluminum and can be placed either inside or outside the greenhouse.

Other screening materials for exterior shading are made of plastic mesh — saran and polypropylene — available in natural, green or black. The amount of shading is predetermined by the weave .

There are sophisticated systems which utilize tracks, rollers and rails built into the greenhouse frame. These systems can be operated by hand or motorized. Some materials also insulate to conserve heat and thereby reduce energy consumption.

Some trial and error may be necessary because no system is ideal for every set of conditions. ❦

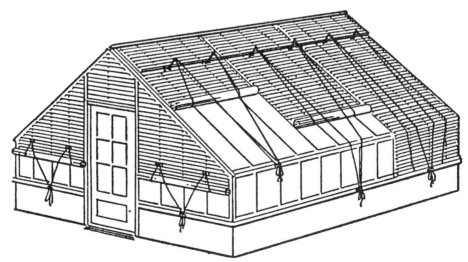

Slat shading. All of the shades can be rolled up and down the roof except those over the ventilating sash and upper part of the gable ends which are fixed with brass buttons.

LABOR SAVING EQUIPMENT

John W. Bartok, Jr.

A hobby greenhouse can be operated with a few basic tools: trowel, knife, pruning shears, pails and hose.

In addition to these standard items you might consider specialized labor-saving equipment. Some chores can be done better with a machine, leaving you more time for other activities. Greenhouse suppliers sell most of the equipment described below.

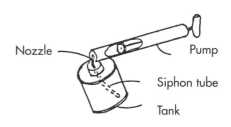

Intermittent hand sprayer

Preparation of Growing Media

Growing media can be purchased ready-to-use or mixed in custom batches. Soil, peat, vermiculite, perlite, lime and fertilizer are the usual components of growing media. A soil shredder can be used to prepare topsoil, loosen baled peat and to mix the components. Shredders are available in capacities beginning at about four cubic yards per hour. They are powered by either an electric motor or with a gas engine. A small portable

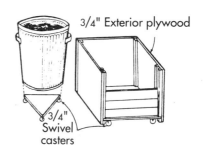

Storage bins for growing media

Concrete or soil mixer   Shredder   Four wheel cart   Double wheel cart

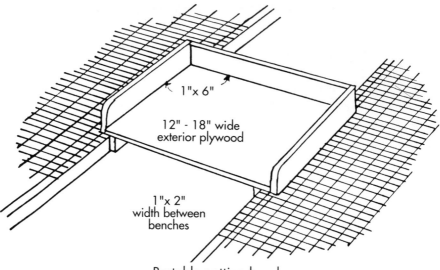

1"x 6"

12" - 18" wide
exterior plywood

1"x 2"
width between
benches

Portable potting bench

concrete mixer is an excellent soil and peatlite mixer. A one-half horsepower electric motor or two horsepower gas engine can be used to power it. A small screen is handy for removing stones and clumps from soil and is simple to make. It can be folded and stored in the headhouse or garage.

Before it is used, soil should be pasteurized to kill disease organisms, pests, and weeds. Heating is the most common and effective method used. A temperature of 140 degrees F for two hours or 180 degrees F for 30 minutes will destroy most disease organisms and weeds. Best results are obtained if the soil or mix is loose and slightly moist at the time of pasteurization. To conserve energy, only the soil needs to be pasteurized. It can then be mixed with peat, vermiculite, perlite or other disease-free components. An electric roaster works well for pasteurizing small amounts of soil. It will do about one flat at a time. Small commercial soil pasteurizers that process one-eighth and one-fourth cubic yard per batch are available. These also operate on electricity and use from six to 12

kilowatt hours per cubic yard.

It is important that soil or mix be stored in containers or in an area where it will not be re-contaminated. The commercially prepared peat-vermiculite mixes are usually stored in their shipping containers until used.

Plant Treatment

Battery-powered and electric seeders aid in seeding. Seed is poured into the scoop and held over the bed or flat. The unit vibrates to feed the seed evenly.

Heating pads, and mats under the soil mix in the bench, provide additional heat for the propagation of cuttings and seedlings. They are available in several sizes. A built-in thermostat controls the temperature level.

The effectiveness of an insecticide or fungicide depends to a large extent on the thorough application of the material. A hand atomizer is commonly used to apply insecticides to small areas. They are available in capacities from one-half pint to two quarts. This sprayer is inexpensive so several may be purchased, one for each type of spray material used.

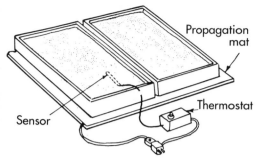

A propagation heat mat can provide the ideal temperature for seed germination.

The compressed air sprayer provides better atomization and spray coverage, especially to the underside of leaves. It is available in capacities from one to five gallons. Since these sprayers are not equipped with an agitator, they must be shaken frequently when wettable powders are sprayed. The plunger-type duster is commonly used to apply pesticides in powder form.

Materials Handling

Single- and double-wheel carts are handy in the home greenhouse when materials need to be moved. Look for large wheels for easy rolling, and make sure the cart is narrow enough to go through the door.

Watering and Misting

Daily hand watering with a garden hose is the most common watering system. Short hoses and several faucets are more convenient than one long hose. You should probably install more than one faucet if the greenhouse is longer than 12 feet. Water breakers attached to the hose will keep soil from being compacted or washed out of the pot or bench. Water potted plants until water begins to flow from the drainage hole. More water will only saturate the soil or reduce the amount of air in the soil; air, as well as water and fertilizer, is necessary

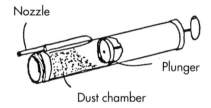

Plunger duster

for good plant growth. Plants should be segregated in the greenhouse according to their water needs as well as their growth cycles. Cacti should be separated from moisture-loving subtropical plants, for example.

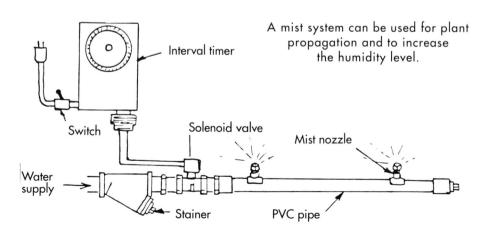

A mist system can be used for plant propagation and to increase the humidity level.

Plants should be watered in the morning so they can dry before evening. Water droplets will cause spotting on some plants and increase fungus disease. A watering can is particularly handy for watering potted plants in a small greenhouse. The spout, with sprinkler head removed, easily reaches beneath plant leaves to water the soil.

Automated watering systems are very convenient for the busy gardener. Plastic nozzles are used to water plants grown in benches. A convenient system uses a polyethylene pipe clamped, or laid along both sides of the bench. Nozzles that spray in a half circle (180 degrees) are inserted along the pipe.

The spaghetti-tube system conveniently waters potted plants. The thin tubes are inserted into a main, one half-inch diameter, polyethylene tube that runs down the center of the bench. Tubes are held in place with a lead weight, a short piece of one half-inch polyethylene tubing, or are tied to a label stake.

A time switch wired to a solenoid valve automates these systems. Some experimentation is needed to decide how long the water should run. The amount of water needed will depend on the season and light and temperature conditions.

A line strainer should be used with any automatic watering system. The strainer filters out any sand or dirt that might clog up the small holes in the nozzles or tubes.

In winter, some plants may not grow well when watered with cold water. The next day's water supply can be stored in a

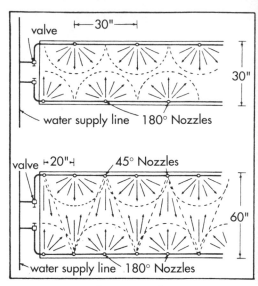

Layouts for plastic nozzle watering systems. Automated watering saves time for other projects.

tank or other container so it will warm to room temperature. If you use a hose or automated system, a hot water line and mixing valve can be installed.

Overhead mixing increases humidity and cools the greenhouse. High humidities are particularly important for rooting cuttings or, in some cases, germinating seed. Misting nozzles, controlled with a time switch, produce a fine spray to keep humidity high. Nozzles are normally mounted 24 to 30 inches above the bench and spaced four feet apart. Water pressure of 30 to 60 pounds per square inch is required for proper operation. Usually the nozzles are timed to operate at a ratio of one on to 60 off, such as six seconds on and six minutes off. Air movement, temperature, and water pressure will modify this ratio. The timer controls a solenoid valve and a day-night timer or manual switch turns off the system at night. A line strainer is essential to avoid plugging the nozzles. 🌰

Drip hose
Capillary mat

Capillary mat watering

GREENHOUSE BENCHES

MIRANDA SMITH

Benches are most useful in greenhouses or areas devoted to seedling or potted ornamental production. The traditional bench design looks like a long, slatted-board table with a one- or three-inch lip. Slats allow excess water to drain. Nonetheless, protect wooden benches

MIRANDA SMITH, *North Troy, VT, has been growing and working in greenhouses since she was a child. She is the author of* **Greenhouse Gardening** *published by Rodale Press.*

with a preservative (see "Tips for Long-Lasting Wooden Structures").

I prefer to make benches from wooden two by four frames covered with bench mesh, a strong metal screening available from greenhouse suppliers. It is wonderful material: strong, lightweight, easy to sterilize and non-shading. Good wire cutters or a welding torch are the only tools that will cut it. You will need U-shaped nails to attach the mesh to the frames. Turn the benches so that project-

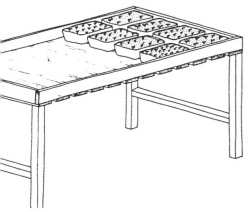

SLATTED BENCH:
This greenhouse workhorse is a great place to locate seedlings and potted ornamentals.
The slats allow water to drain away.

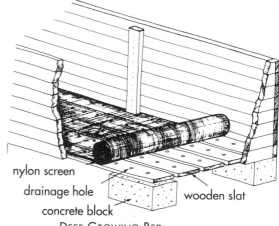

nylon screen
drainage hole
concrete block
wooden slat

DEEP GROWING BED:
You must provide plants with good drainage and air circulation. In this bed the open-spaced slats, drainage holes and concrete blocks ensure that water will escape and air will circulate.

ing two-by-fours form a lip. If you plan to use heavy pots on a wire bench, and cross-supports at three-foot intervals.

The most stable and versatile legs for benches are wooden two by four sawhorses. But almost anything else will work as well. Some people use a couple of plastic or wooden crates while others pile up cinder blocks. Height is determined by convenience; benches aren't solid enough to interfere with air circulation. I like to work with benches about three feet off the ground. At this height the root zone is quite warm, and besides, my back doesn't hurt after a long day of potting or transplanting.

Almost every greenhouse can use at least one bench. Many herbs and orna-mentals grow in small pots as well as, or better than, they do in a bed. Benches also make very good starting areas for seedling flats because it is so easy to transform them into propagating chambers. The space under a bench is a handy storage area. Fill it with boxes of pots, buckets of soil mix ingredients, and jugs of liquid seaweed and fish emulsion. In the fall it is easy to clear all of the pots off the bench and use it for drying rack for onions or a curing area for a winter squash. Draped with a sheet of polyethylene, benches make good vegetable and herb drying areas. 🌱

Reprinted from *Greenhouse Gardening* © 1985 by Miranda Smith. Permission granted by Rodale Press, Inc. Emmaus, PA.

The benches at Longwood Gardens are made of metal with a mesh cover to assist in drainage.

A greenhouse made of wood is attractive and will last
if protective measures are taken.

TIPS FOR LONG-LASTING WOODEN STRUCTURES

MIRANDA SMITH

Naturally durable woods such as cedar and cypress, or lumber treated to resist decay, can prolong the life of wooden structures. Pressure-treated lumber is often used in greenhouses. Since it has been treated with arsenic compounds, the safest way to use it is as part of the structural frame. Don't use it for containers that will come in contact with the soil. Cedar and cypress, which naturally resist decay, are the best choices for growing beds. These woods can be expensive, but perhaps you can locate other growers in the area who would be willing to join forces to place a large order that would qualify for a reduced rate.

If you can't locate these woods, or if they're not available, you can use a wood preservative to treat beds and containers. The safest preservative is copper naphthenate (sold under the trade name Cuprinol). It is very effective, and while it poses no harm to plants or people, copper naphthenate does kill soil fungi and bacteria for a brief period of time after application. It also releases volatile toxic solvents as it dries. When you use copper naphthenate on lumber for beds, let the boards weather outside for a few weeks before exposing them to soil.

Try not to use paints or preservatives inside the greenhouse when plants are growing there. If you must do so, wait until a week when the weather is warm enough to leave the greenhouse open all night. Vent as completely as possible during the entire time that the paint or preservative is drying...and then add a few days for extra measure.

While I'm insistent upon treating all wooden parts of a greenhouse structure with preservatives, I use beds made of untreated wood, lined with plastic film. These beds might rot a few years before preserved wood will, but they pose no threat to soil life. I use six-mil construction-grade polyethylene stapled to the sides of the beds or to any wooden containers, I never use it to cover the bottoms because that would prevent water from draining away. 🌱

Reprinted from Greenhouse Gardening © 1985 by Miranda Smith. Permission granted by Rodale Press, Inc., Emmaus, PA 18049.

WATERING A GREENHOUSE

TOVAH MARTIN

There is no melody as sweet as the gentle tinkling of water as it passes from hose to pot. Without a doubt, the sound of water splashing over one thirsty plant and another is music to any grower's ear. A well-watered greenhouse is heaven on earth, whereas a poorly watered house can be hellish.

Watering is the greatest chore in the greenhouse, and also the most relentless job that a grower must perform. Day after day, week after week, month after month, a greenhouse must be watered. Even on the darkest, cloudiest day there is always a dry pot here or there. In mid-winter, the plants can wait until tomorrow. In mid-summer, their thirst can scarcely go unquenched another hour.

Although watering is definitely a chore, it is much less arduous in modern greenhouses than it was a century ago, thanks to 20th century technology. Until this century, water was collected in cisterns from roof gutters along the outside greenhouse frame. The system worked marvelously during rainy seasons. But, in times of drought, it did not function as effectively. When the cisterns failed, growers resorted to hauling water from nearby ponds. On a hot, dry day, as soon as they had completed one round of hauling and watering, it was time to start at the beginning and rewater the entire house.

Fortunately we now have running, piped-in water available, and every greenhouse should be equipped with water pipes. However, even with an endless supply of water at your beck and call, watering is still the ruin of many greenhouse collections. Watering may seem like a simple procedure, but every year hundreds of plants perish due to faulty watering.

No one can tell you exactly how to water a greenhouse—it is a skill that must be learned through trial and error. Anyone who waters according to a strict schedule is doomed to failure—Mother Nature simply does not go by the clock. During a rainy week your plants may only require watering twice. But on a bright, sunny week your greenhouse will probably need watering both morning and afternoon every day. Even these examples are not as simple as they seem. On a cold, rainy day the heating system might dry out plants to the point of wilting if watering is neglected. Similarly, in the summer, a cooling system might prevent the plants from drying out. Vigilance is the only truly effective method of scheduling weekly watering.

Basically, you should water when a plant is dry to the touch. Experienced growers can tell a dry plant at a glance. For those who are new at the job, feel the soil by digging a finger down about one-half inch and test it for moisture. When

When watering, allow the hose to run in a gentle stream.

it is dry to the touch, give the plant a drink.

When watering, allow the hose to run with a gentle stream into the pot, directing the water with your finger, or you might try adding a wand or sprinkling attachment to your nozzle. If the water splashes out of the pot or loosens soil on the surface, it is running too strongly.

When giving a plant its drink, fill the pot to the rim with water. Every plant should have a one-fourth to one inch (depending upon the size of the pot) lip without soil, left specifically for holding water. Only fill the lip once, do not allow it to soak in and then, fill it again. And always water in the morning so that moisture on the leaves will dry before sundown.

One of the cardinal sins in greenhouse growing is overwatering. Everyone has done it once in a while — especially with their favorite plants. It is difficult not to kill a plant with kindness. But, it is far better to underwater than to overwater. When you overwater, you saturate the air pockets around the roots with moisture, leaving the roots suffocating for oxygen. The plant can fall prey to a host of ills including root rot and other related maladies. In fact, a slight wilt stimulates bud formation in many tropical plants. When it comes to watering, most plants thrive on neglect.

In general, you will find that plants in clay pots require more frequent watering than those in plastic containers. Hanging pots usually require twice as much water as plants set on the ground. And plants that are pot-bound and need repotting cry for water continually and wilt pathetically between drinks.

Certain plants require individual care when watering. Gesneriads (members of the African Violet family) prefer warm water. You might give them their drink early in the morning if your water pipes are warmed by heating pipes. Gesneriads also object to wet foliage, so take care to water the soil and not their leaves.

In addition to water, the hose can also dispense fertilizer at the same time, thus accomplishing two chores at one time. Many growers prefer to fertilize with dilute solutions (usually one teaspoon to one gallon of water) every time they water. If this method is followed, the precaution should be taken to flush residues from the plants every fifth watering with clear water. Hose attachments that fit into the spigot are available, running a slender take-up tube into a bucket filled with partially diluted fertilizer. Not only are you providing your plants with refreshment, you are also nourishing them.

Proper greenhouse watering is rarely mastered overnight. However, once you have learned the ropes, it comes naturally. Although it is a chore, it can be an enjoyable job. Watering is both therapeutic and fulfilling. A tremendous sense of accomplishment accompanies a grower as he or she watches each plant gratefully drink its share and instantly perk up.

Sweet peas growing on a tripod.

GROWING VEGETABLES IN THE HOME GREENHOUSE

Karen K. Rane

Raising vegetables to maturity in a greenhouse when conditions are unfavorable for gardening outdoors provides a considerable challenge. However, the rewards are well worth the effort. With a little knowledge, patience and experience, anyone can grow a variety of garden-fresh vegetables in a small home greenhouse long after the summer is past.

Plant Selection

In addition to your personal taste preferences, deciding which vegetable crops to grow will depend on your greenhouse

Dr. Karen Rane, *Waltham, MA is an Extension technician at the University of Massachusetts Suburban Experiment Station. Her specialty is plant pathology.*

environment (especially the temperature and light levels) and the space available. The vegetables that are most suitable for greenhouse production include leafy vegetables, radishes, cucumbers, peppers and tomatoes.

In many cases, certain cultivars have been developed specifically for commercial greenhouse cultivation. In addition, maximum use of limited greenhouse space can be accomplished by growing cultivars developed for containers or small gardens. These tend to have a more compact growing habit than other varieties and mature more rapidly.

Temperature and Light

Vegetables require the same light and temperature conditions regardless of whether they are grown outdoors in summer or in the greenhouse in winter. During the winter, light and temperature can become limiting factors in vegetable production, especially in northern latitudes. It is often difficult to predict the time to maturity of greenhouse vegetables. When planning their planting schedules, many greenhouse gardeners fail to take into account that it may take a crop twice as long to mature when it is grown indoors.

Seedlings germinate and grow rapidly under warm conditions. Heating cables, which provide bottom heat to seedling flats, reduce the germination time significantly, especially in the winter months. However, to prevent legginess, bottom heat should be eliminated as soon as the seedlings emerge.

Optimum temperatures for growing vegetables to maturity vary according to the particular crop. Cool-season crops such as lettuce, spinach and peas grow best when night temperatures range from 50 to 60 degrees F, and day temperatures range from 65 to 75 degrees F. Warm-season crops such as tomatoes, peppers and cucumbers need night temperatures of 70 to 80 degrees F. While some greenhouses may have cool and warm spots allowing for the production of crops with varying temperature requirements, it is usually more practical to choose crops according to the minimum night temperature maintained in the greenhouse.

Temperatures may also be a limiting factor during the summer months, when cooling the greenhouse becomes a problem. Excessive heat build-up can be controlled with cooling systems and shading. But many gardeners, especially those in southern areas, find it easier to close down their greenhouse during the summer.

The duration of light is also important for vegetable growth. Some crops, such as beans and peas, are stimulated to produce flowers and fruit under conditions of increasing day length. This requirement can be met by using supplemental light during winter, or growing the crop in early spring to take advantage of the naturally increasing day length.

Light quality and intensity are equally important. In general, vegetables grown for foliage can tolerate light of less intensity than vegetables grown for fruit production. Natural light intensity can be increased with supplemental lighting. However, it is less expensive to grow crops adapted to the prevailing light conditions of the season. Tomatoes, peppers and cucumbers will produce relatively good crops in spring and fall. Whereas, during the cloudy, short days of winter, greenhouse growers in northern climates will have more success with leafy vegetables. Those greenhouse gardeners who reside in southern locales generally have more flexibility with regard to vegetable production because light levels in these areas do not vary as greatly with the changing seasons.

Growing Methods

Starting vegetable plants from seed in a pathogen-free growing medium is the best way to produce plants for the greenhouse. Plants transplanted from outdoor vegetable gardens often harbor insects, weeds and disease-causing microorganisms which will continue to cause problems in the greenhouse environment and spread to other plants.

Advanced planning is necessary to have vegetable plants ready to be transplanted for greenhouse production. For example, tomato seed should be sown in late June in the Northeast for fall greenhouse production, and the spring tomato crop should be started in early January.

Ground beds

Vegetables can be planted in the soil on

which the greenhouse stands if organic matter and other amendments are added to the existing soil. This method allows tall crops grown on strings or trellises to attain their maximum height. In addition, root room is also maximized.

Optimally, the soil should be pasteurized to reduce root-rotting microorganisms. Steam lines can be built into the ground bed to allow the soil to be periodically steam-pasteurized, but this is not always practical.

Bag culture

An alternative to a ground bed is relatively recent practice of growing vegetable crops directly in bags of soilless media placed on the greenhouse floor. Plants are inserted in holes cut in the top surface of the bag, and drainage holes are cut in the bottom surface. The problem of soil pasteurization is avoided (commercial soilless mixes are free of root pests) while the use of maximum greenhouse height is maintained. A three-cubic-foot bag of peatlite mix can accommodate two large tomato plants. The bags are discarded after use to avoid root rot problems.

Containers

Containerized vegetable production is probably most adaptable to the home greenhouse, especially if the greenhouse has some sort of bench structure. There is an unlimited array of containers suitable for growing vegetables. The containers should be large enough to provide adequate room for root growth. In general, a minimum depth of nine inches and a minimum diameter of 12 inches is necessary.

Drainage holes are essential. Containers can be constructed of clay, plastic, concrete or wood. Deep wooden boxes are especially convenient for growing root crops.

Containerized vegetables thrive in a well-drained growing medium, whether it be a soilless mix or a soil-based medium. The pH should be maintained at 6.5 to 6.8. Most importantly, all components of a growing medium should be free of pathogens. If field soil is used in a homemade mix, it should be pasteurized for 30 minutes at 180 degrees F.

Special Greenhouse Problems

In the garden, insects pollinate flowers of vegetables grown for their fruit. But this task must be performed by the gardener when vegetables are grown in a greenhouse. Tomato, pepper, bean and pea plants can be shaken to distribute pollen. A small brush, inserted into each flower, can also be used. Cucumbers and squash must be hand-pollinated with a brush, since these vegetables produce male and female flowers separately. An exception to this rule is the European cucumber cultivars which are bred specifically for greenhouse production.

High humidity in greenhouses can encourage diseases that would not ordinarily cause problems on outdoor vegetables. Certain fungus diseases such as leaf mold on tomato plants and Botrytis blight on lettuce leaves can become severe in greenhouse environments.

Greenhouse vegetables are often subject to increased handling during transplanting, staking, pruning and pollination, which can spread disease-causing agents such as tobacco mosaic virus. However, simple sanitation practices, such as removing plant debris, discarding sickly plants and washing hands often while handling corps, can reduce the spread of disease. Controlling humidity levels through ventilation and adequate plant spacing will also help to control diseases in the greenhouse.

Vegetables grown in the greenhouse are subject to the same insect pests that attack greenhouse ornamentals. Careful attention to insect control is necessary for successful greenhouse vegetable gardening. Insecticides should be used with caution and according to the label directions, especially since the crop will be consumed.

Some Common Greenhouse Vegetable Crops: Tomatoes

There are many cultivars of this crop which perform well in the greenhouse. 'Vendor', 'Caruso', 'Jumbo' and 'Dumbo' are a few of the cultivars developed specifically for greenhouse production, but many garden cultivars also produce a good greenhouse harvest. Choose disease-resistant cultivars.

Tomatoes can be planted as a fall or spring crop, but the harvest will be much greater in the spring. Greenhouse tomatoes may take 100 to 140 days to reach maturity from seed, and need warm temperatures (60 to 65 degrees F at night to 70 to 75 degrees F during the day) for best production.

Ground beds, bag culture and large containers are all suitable for growing tomatoes; and mulches can be used to maintain constant moisture levels. Young plants should not be over-fertilized, since this encourages soft growth, although tomato plants do require higher nutrient levels when fruit begins to develop. Tomatoes should be pruned and trained to develop a single stem, and supported with stakes or trellises. Tomato flowers are self-fertile, but the plants must be shaken to distribute the pollen.

Cucumbers

Cucumbers are a warm-season crop, and require 65 degrees F nights and up to 85 degrees F days for optimal growth. Bright light is also needed for most cultivars, making this crop more productive during the long days in spring and summer in northern areas. 'Burpee Hybrid', 'Spacemaster' and 'Victory Hybrid' are garden cultivars that also grow well in the greenhouse if hand pollinated. European cultivars which need no pollination include 'Sandra', 'Super Sandra', 'Toska 70' and 'Superator'. 'Kosura' and 'Pandex' are two European cucumber cultivars developed to tolerate lower light and temperature conditions.

Cucumbers mature in 55 to 70 days from seed, and are "heavy feeders", requiring relatively high nutrient levels as their fruit develops. For maximum production, European cucumbers must be trained to grow vertically with stakes or trellises. Other cucumber cultivars can also be grown in this manner to conserve greenhouse space.

Lettuce

Lettuce is a cool-season crop, growing best when night temperatures are 50 to 55 degrees F and day temperatures do not exceed 70 degrees F. In general, looseleaf and loosehead (buttercrunch) lettuce types are best suited to greenhouse production. Cultivars that tolerate the low-light levels typical of northern winters include 'Arctic King', 'Captain', 'Diamante' and 'Grand Rapids'.

Spring conditions in the greenhouse are ideal for most lettuce cultivars. But for late spring or early summer production, choose cultivars that are heat tolerant and slow to bolt, such as 'Boston Bibb', 'Green Ice' and 'Slo-Bolt'.

Lettuce plants have shallow root systems, and can be grown successfully in relatively small containers. Lettuce should be fertilized sparingly, but it should be frequently watered to prevent its shallow root system from drying out.

Lettuce can be harvested 55 to 80 days after it is sown. In addition, the supply of this vegetable can be extended by successive plantings, or by harvesting outer leaves while leaving the plant intact. 🌶

Camellia

GROWING COOL-LOVING PLANTS IN A 19TH CENTURY GREENHOUSE

HENRIETTA LIGHT

The historic greenhouses on the Lyman Estate in Waltham, Massachusetts give the indoor gardening enthusiast an interesting sense of the past. The greenhouse complex, as old as any known to be still

HENRIETTA P. LIGHT *is the horticulturist at "The Vale," an historic 19th century greenhouse maintained by the Society for the Preservation of New England Antiquities. She is also a garden and landscape designer and a horticultural consultant.*

standing in the United States, was built by Theodore Lyman, a Boston merchant, at his summer home which was built between 1793 and 1798. The estate is preserved and the greenhouses kept in use by the Society for the Preservation of New England Antiquities (SPNEA).

The dwelling house was placed in a meadow between a small river to the south and a gentle wooded slope to the north. A wooded knoll to the east completes a sense of place which made "The Vale" an appropriate name.

Between 1795 and 1800 Lyman had a 38-foot greenhouse built into the south-facing slope beyond the back of the house site. The greenhouse was heated by fuel burned in a rectangular metal fire box which fitted into the western end of a horizontal flue. This flue ran in front of a raised bed to a chimney at the eastern end. At present, this house is preserved, but it is not in use.

The next greenhouse was built about 1804 for growing citrus, pineapples, bananas and forced native fruit. It was one of many such greenhouses in the Boston area, where an aristocracy of successful merchants showed energetic and often scholarly interest in growing exotic fruit and improving native varieties. Plants were grown in the south-facing half of the house, and the back wall of the plant room divided it from storage space on the northern side which acted as a buffer against the cold. The builders did not know that 180 years later such a structure would be called "solar."

Around 1820 a greenhouse was added for camellias. In the relatively few years since the camellia had arrived in the New World in 1797, the lovely blossoms had caught the imagination of some very ambitious growers, amateur and professional. We have no evidence that Theodore Lyman was involved in growing and hybridizing, but he certainly patronized the culture of those exquisite novelties, and made possible a superb setting in which to grow them.

The camellia house was set against, or replaced, a 75-foot section of garden wall to the east of the fruit house. Eventually, 45 feet of that wall was glassed in to form a rose house. A fifth greenhouse was built in 1935 for the purpose of growing cut flowers. It extended to the north behind the rose house.

Contemporary greenhouse enthusi-asts are indebted to the four generations of Lymans whose continued interest in horticulture ensured the preservation and maintenance of the greenhouses. The estate, diminished from its original 400 acres to 27.5, was given to SPNEA in 1951.

Although most of the original exotic and native fruits are gone from the greenhouses, the grapes planted in 1870 are still thriving. Roses are gone from the center house which is now used for orchids and other tropical and semi-tropical plants. As for the camellias, there are thirteen thriving trees which are more than 100 years old and have reached heights between 15 and 25 feet!

The camellias are housed in a 15 by 90 foot greenhouse. It is a lean-to-design built against a brick wall with top and side vents, manually operated, running the length of the house. The upper glass of this house (and throughout the greenhouse complex) is now insulated with a polyethylene bubble, two layers inflated by air pumped by an electric motor through plastic tubing. The camellia trees are set permanently in large, three foot-square planters formed in the front by a vertical low wall of concrete two-feet high. This parallels the back wall of the greenhouse three feet behind. The trees are set four and one-half feet apart in soil between these front and back walls. Redwood partitions form side walls.

The camellia collection is truly the showpiece of the greenhouses. `Alba plena' starts its distinctively long blooming season in late October. The other varieties follow, each at its own time, creating a peak of bloom in February. 'Peppermint' and 'Virgin's Blush' are still blooming in April. The blossoms are pink, white or red, two and one-half to four inches in diameter and often appear on almost every growing tip of a tree.

The Lyman Estate is open to the public for a small admission charge. Visitors

54

who come in from New England's damp or bitter cold, from gray days of early darkness or winter rain and mud, take great delight in the winter garden created by the trees. The blossoming camellias inspire the frequent query, "Can I grow these?"

The answer lies, as with most plant culture, in understanding the growing conditions of the plant's native habitat. Camellias originate in thin woodlands in coastal China and offshore islands. They enjoy abundant rainfall, high humidity, and well-drained soil. They can withstand high summer temperatures and light frost in winter as long as there are no wide fluctuations in daily temperature. In a greenhouse, they require good light but no bright sun, 65 to 70 percent humidity, a 20 degree F day-night temperature range, ideally 60 degrees during the day and 40 degrees at night (the colder the temperature, the longer the blossoms last), well-drained soil with a pH of about 5.5, and good ventilation. Come summer, the pots should be sunk in the ground outdoors in filtered light or semishade.

If not controlled, camellias will eventually grow too large for easy handling. When their roots have filled a 12-inch pot, do not move the plant on to a larger pot, but root prune instead. This is an alarming process for the novice, but it is harmless to a plant with a good root system. Root pruning may be accomplished any time between late winter and early spring, before the air is so warm that the plant would be stressed. Cut away an inch and a half of soil from the sides of the root ball with a long, sharp knife, and cut three pie-shaped wedges from the sides of the bottom. Then put fresh soil into the old pot, positioning it to replace the wedges. Place the trimmed root ball in the pot and add fresh soil around the sides. Selectively prune the top growth of the plant in proportion to the amount taken away from the roots. Water well and keep the plant in a shady place for several days to minimize water loss. Two months after root pruning, use cottonseed meal or any all-purpose container fertilizer sparingly.

The cool greenhouse in which camellias thrive is one of the most manageable and rewarding of indoor growing environments. One of its primary virtues is the fact that there is less insect proliferation when temperatures are low. At the Lyman greenhouses, insecticides are only used as a last resort. Instead, a population of predacious spiders and wasps keep aphids, whiteflies and mealybugs at bay. Insecticidal soap is used throughout the greenhouse once a week. Watering is necessary less frequently at cool temperatures. Blossoms last longer. (Camellia blossoms may last a month!) And repotting is also less often required.

Many cool-loving plants share the camellias' affinity for low nighttime temperatures. The plants listed on the following page are grown at "The Vale" in a greenhouse that goes to 45 degrees F on many winter nights. 🌿

RHODODENDRON INDICUM Once triggered into bloom by the cool nights in the greenhouse, these lushly blooming beauties will last well in the house if kept well watered.

BEGONIA X ERYTHROPHYLLA, B. ERYTHROPHYLLA 'HELIX', B. SCHARFFII Grow these on the dry side in coldest weather, to prevent rotting.

CAMELLIA JAPONICA This is the variety of the old trees at "The Vale." Buds of the showy blooms start to form in mid-summer, and open between October and May, depending on variety.

C. RETICULATA This is a species with a lankier growth habit than the above, with veined – "reticulated" – leaves. The larger blossomed plants are less vigorous and adaptable than japonicas.

C. SASANQUA This is more vigorous and fast growing than japonica, and more tolerant of cold and of bright light. Most sasanquas bloom between August and January, setting more buds than japonicas or reticulatas. The one drawback is that the delicately scented flowers shatter in a few days.

CLIVIA MINIATA Keep very cool and dry until early March, when thorough watering will trigger bloom.

CYMBIDIUM These are terrestrial orchids whose blossoms appear between November and May, lasting eight or nine weeks! Look for miniatures to save space.

JASMINUM NUDIFLORUM JASMINUM POLYANTHUM Bear yellow and pale pink flowers respectively, bare-leaved, in mid-winter. Until buds are set in fall or early winter, withhold artificial light after sundown or cover plant if there must be light.

JASMINUM PRIMULINUM The yellow blossoms often mistaken for forced forsythia because of bloom time and color.

LYGODIUM JAPONICUM Japanese climbing fern. This offers an interesting texture, with its trailing, curling tracery of stems and leaves for which wires or trellis should be provided. Give plenty of water.

MUEHLENBECKIA COMPLEXA Maidenhair vine. Another plant which provides delicate texture with its wiry stems and small tidy leaves.

OSMANTHUS FRAGRANS Sweet olive or tea olive. Inconspicuous cream-colored blossoms have heavy fragrance September through May. Grows slowly into a small tree.

PELARGONIUMS OF ALL KINDS These are the geraniums of our window boxes and summer gardens, as well as dwarf-growing types and scented leaved ones (lime, lemon, peppermint, and many others) with small flowers. Let dry out between waterings, and be scrupulous about not watering in cloudy weather. This is a general rule of thumb in cool greenhouse culture, unless a plant is so dried out as to be wilting.

PRIMULA SPP. Primroses. Beware that some people are allergic to the leaves of *P. obconica, malacoides* and *chinensis* particularly.

ROSMARINUS OFFICINALIS Rosemary. Lovely in texture and growth habit, this is a continuing source for fresh flavoring and provides a pleasing scent when touched.

STREPTOCARPUS SPP. Cape primrose. Do not overwater these purple, lavender, and white blooming relatives of the African violet.

TIBOUCHINA SEMIDECANDRA Cut back in April and pinch tips relentlessly until August to attain a maximum of the large flat, rich purple blooms in late fall and early winter.

SCHLUMBERGERA TRUNCATA Thanksgiving cactus.

S. BRIDGESII Christmas cactus. Cool temperature, no artificial light after sunset, and withheld water in October should assure a good show of bloom.

BULBS FOR FORCING: FREESIA, ANEMONE CORONARIA These tender bulbs should be planted in eight inch or deeper pots. The small bulbs belie their need for root space.

HARDY BULBS Tulips, narcissus, crocus, bulbous iris. Cool greenhouse conditions are ideal for a long lasting show. Your dealer carries varieties specified for forcing.

HEDERA SPP. Ivy

SOLEIROLIA SOLEIROLII (HELXINE SOLEIROLII) Baby's tears

CYMBALARIA MURALIS Kenilworth ivy.

All of these plants can be used in low pots on benches or floor in front of larger pots, as a kind of mock ground cover to add a graceful appearance to your winter garden.

THE EVOLUTION OF A COOL GREENHOUSE FROM BUILDING TO BULBS

JOHN BARSTOW

On a dull-day in mid-February John Gilmore's greenhouse is a welcome sight. There is a tiny bright space jammed with the colors and scents of scores of familiar spring flowers.

Gilmore's greenhouse is a stage on which he produces a succession of glorious bloom over five gloomy months, from November through March. In any given winter week he is tending a dozen different flowering plants. Crimson and white amaryllis, drifts of butter-yellow and scarlet freesias, narcissus of many sizes and forms, and bright tulips cover practically every inch of the small bench. Tucked in among these—behind them, on crowded shelves above them, on the floor below them—are pots of pale pink, lilac, and white hyacinths; trays of lily of the valley and impatiens; cyclamen and clivias. Baskets of lantana hang from the metal rafters.

All of this midwinter color is choreographed in a seven- by 11-foot Lord & Burnham lean-to greenhouse that John Gilmore, a trial attorney, built onto his yellow clapboard house in Cambridge,

JOHN BARSTOW *is an editor of Atlantic Monthly Press and the former managing editor of* **Horticulture**.

Massachusetts. In 1982 when the greenhouse was constructed, Gilmore had thrift on his mind as much as blossoms. "Originally I'd planned to generate some heat for the house. But I got much more interested in gardening and much less interested in heating the house." So much so that within the year Gilmore had not only abandoned notions of economical passive-solar heat, he had purchased for the greenhouse its own furnace, a small gas-fired model installed in the basement not 10 feet from the big oil burner.

Of the energy-efficient double-glazing he had specified to the manufacturer, Gilmore ruefully comments, "Yes, there's less heat loss, but there's also a reduction in light to my plants." So much for thrift. His decision to give the greenhouse its own heat source is emblematic of his horticultural evolution. Gilmore started with modest aims suited to his limited know-how, but was quick to plunge deeper as gardening became more compelling, learning as he proceeded.

The greenhouse got off to a haphazard start. Gilmore and a friend dug the four to five-foot deep foundation hole by hand in October. A contractor poured the footings and built the cinder-block

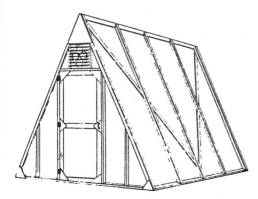

Plans such as this one and several to follow are available from: University of Connecticut. Plan no. 238, A-frame home greenhouse

foundation just before frost set in. Then Gilmore filled the hole with crushed rock, the heat sink for his passive-solar heating scheme. Once all was in readiness, the manufacturer sent a crew to erect the house itself.

Gilmore's haste to close in the greenhouse before winter made that first season "a bit of a trial. I had no water, no heat, no floor, and no access except through windows off the living room. That spring I put in the French doors." In putting in a floor he turned his idle heat sink to advantage. Gilmore decided to leave the crushed rock exposed under the three-foot wide bench he had built against the outside wall. He finished the remainder of the floor, about half the area, in terra-cotta tiles. This arrangement affords him a clean area to stand on, while the relatively small quantity of water he uses drains through the rock. Bit by bit the greenhouse came together. "After six months of going crazy carrying water I put in a water line," says Gilmore. Eventually he installed not only running water but a mixer that combines hot and cold water in the basement and delivers tepid water to the tap in the greenhouse. Another addition, electric outlets, allowed Gilmore to work evenings: "To come home at the end of the day in win-

ter when it's dark, turn on the greenhouse lights, and just water the plants is a joy." Thermostats, one to regulate heat from the gas furnace and a second to regulate ventilation, were installed, and Gilmore's greenhouse had arrived.

John Gilmore's greenhouse is cool. He prefers to grow hardy bulbs and other spring-flowering plants that thrive with a minimum nighttime temperature of 45 degrees and a winter daytime high of 60 degree. Even though the bulbs tolerate slightly lower temperatures, Gilmore maintains a minimum nighttime temperature of 50 degrees in deference to tender perennials like tropical hibiscus. He closely adheres to the 60 degrees maximum temperature, however, since more heat would speed growth and substantially shorten the life of each blossom.

Gilmore's gardening seasons more nearly resemble those of New Zealand than New England. Sometime in August, when gardens (and gardeners) hereabouts are looking a little worn out, Gilmore is setting the stage for his midwinter blitz. That's when he sows his first two or three pots of nasturtium seed. For the next six months, every four weeks, he sows another two or three pots of nastur-

Attached greenhouse (a solar collector), University of Connecticut Plan no. 252

Tulips sprouting after being treated to a cool period.

tiums so that he'll have some of these "filler plants," as he calls them, in bloom right through until summer.

Housekeeping is the next step in his carefully orchestrated chain of events. Before he returns his tender potted perennials to the protection of the greenhouse he scrubs down the works, including glass, walls, floor, bench, shelves, and each of his clay pots. All these being thoroughly cleansed, he sets off an insecticidal bomb in the green-house, closes the doors, and crosses his fingers in hopes for another relatively pest-free year.

Finally, the plants enter the scene. Tender perennials that find a place in his greenhouse include a four-year-old cattleya orchid; two tropical hibiscus that produce saucer-sized scarlet flowers all winter and spring; a jasmine "I've never persuaded to bloom;" a camellia; pelargoniums, cut back and made to bloom again; an azalea; cyclamen, "fabu-

Hyacinths and tulips can be forced for winter color.

lous plants for a cool greenhouse that give me two months of good bloom in winter;" several agapanthus and clivias; lantanas and a venerable rosemary.

The larger potted plants occupy the floor along the wall of the house, where there is somewhat less light and temperatures are slightly cooler. The agapanthuses, which are wintering over in the greenhouse, live beneath the bench, where there is even less light. Every greenhouse has cooler spots, and Gilmore uses his wisely. These established plants needn't occupy the precious growing area on the bench, and they admirably fill out corners that would otherwise be bare. The jasmine and lantana occupy hanging pots.

With the arrival of September comes Gilmore's busy season. He begins potting up the hundreds of bulbs that will bloom through the dark months ahead. In the annual replacement of bulbs, Gilmore is extravagant; he saves few—mostly

61

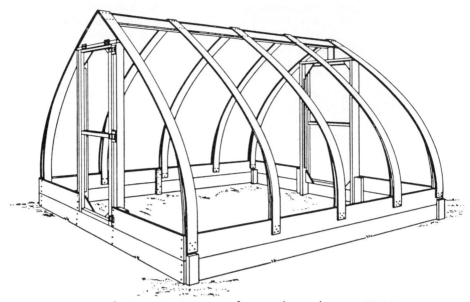

United States Department of Agriculture Plan no. 5946

amaryllis—from year to year, believing that bulbs once forced are not likely to come on strong the second year. The following 90 days are punctuated by weekends down in the basement, where a corner is given over to the implements and ingredients of the potting shed; stacks of terra-cotta pots of every size and description, seedling flats, as well as bales of peat moss, huge bags of perlite, sacks of sterile potting soil and sand.

At the far end of this jumbled corner is a small wooden door that leads through the brick foundation to a dark, cool, low-ceilinged room about six feet wide and twice as long. At its far end another door leads outside. This curious anteroom is the heart of Gilmore's little operation. It is a ready-made root cellar far enough from the cellar proper to provide the cool temperatures he needs to chill his bulbs. On a typical mid-November evening the room contains some 70 clay pots stuffed with bulbs.

Manipulation of light and temperature is the key to tricking plants to do unnatural things, and this is where Gilmore's cold room comes in handy. In it he holds bulbs in darkness at between 45 and 33 degrees F (never below freezing) for anywhere from 10 to 15 weeks, the chilling period required to make hardy bulbs think they've been through winter. During this apparent dormancy they make good root growth, which equips them to produce blossoms once they are moved up into the light. Gilmore also purchases precooled bulbs which are ready to go into the greenhouse in two to four weeks, depending on how long he chooses to hold them in abeyance, and they blossom at least four weeks earlier than other bulbs.

Without this cool room Gilmore would be unable to trick his hundreds of bulbs into blooming over the course of the winter. "It's a little hard to control. I pot them over a long period but, still, when bulbs are showing several inches of growth I can't hold them any longer, I have to bring them up to the greenhouse. Bulbs newly arrived from the cold room go under the bench for a week to acclimate to the warmth and light of the greenhouse.

Once his spring-flowering bulbs begin their display in mid-December Gilmore spends more time in the greenhouse and less in the basement. He has only to water the plants regularly, fertilize occasionally (he top-dresses with an all-purpose fertilizer), keep an eye out for pests, replenish the supply of bulbs as early arrivals fade and another batch is ready to be removed from the cold, and see to it that the temperature stays within bounds. By March lengthening daylight and the higher angle of the sun begin to threaten his collection with too much heat. "In March I begin to use a fan to get the hot air out. A problem with small greenhouses is that temperatures change rapidly."

April and May mark the beginning of the end of Gilmore's greenhouse year. He sows seeds of annuals (impatiens and marigolds, mostly) that will be planted in the garden for summer bloom and gives the house its spring cleaning.

To accomplish all this Gilmore figures he puts in around five hours per week from September through May. Roughly speaking, he spends two hours Monday through Friday watering and generally looking after the plants. The remaining three hours are alloted to weekend tasks like potting bulbs, sowing seed, moving plants in and out of the greenhouse, and spring and fall cleaning.

Summer is "pretty bare bones," he says. "This past year, though, I used it to better advantage. I started tuberous begonias in late spring and they bloomed all summer." So continues John Gilmore's progress. He is always trying new plants, and he is always experimenting with greenhousing. In fact, he has plans for a large porch at the southwest corner of his house. It will be fitted with floor-to-ceiling, double-paned glass. Though he prefers to call it "my glassed-in porch, "it will amount to a conservatory. Needless to say he has great plans for it, but he is proceeding one step at a time. 🌿

REPRINTED COURTESY OF **HORTICULTURE, THE MAG-AZINE OF AMERICAN GARDENING**, 20 PARK PLAZA, SUITE 1220, BOSTON, MA 02116. © 1987, HORTICULTURE PARTNERS.

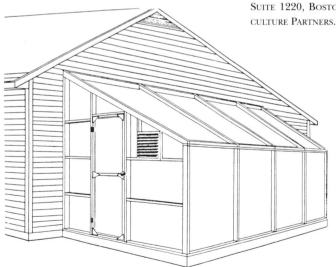

Lean-to greenhouse, University of Connecticut Plan no. 248

CUT FLOWERS FOR COOL GREENHOUSES

JAMES STEVENSON

WITH ASSISTANCE FROM

DEBORAH MATTHEWS

Carnations, chrysanthemums, stocks and snapdragons have been popular as cut flowers for many years. All are relatively long-lasting as cut flowers and all thrive in cold greenhouses that require less

JAMES STEVENSON *is a gardener on a private estate on Long Island, New York.*

energy to heat during the cold months of winter. Although only a handful of plants have attained international fame as cut flowers, there are many more that are equally appropriate.

In our estate greenhouses on Long Island, we work with many cut flowers that can be grown in a cool greenhouse (maintained at 45 to 50 degrees F at

Many of the cut flowers seen in flower markets can be grown in a home greenhouse.

64

night with good unobstructed light, or in an unheated frame that can be covered with a layer of heavy mil clear plastic. In particular, we have had success with the following cut flowers.

Annual *Gypsophila* or baby's breath is easily grown in soil-filled flats or other shallow wooden boxes. Seed planted thinly, or thinned after germination, sprouts readily and grows quickly. Starting a new flat with seed every two or three weeks from January 1st will provide continous cutting material for many weeks in spring.

Another highly recommended cut flower is *Saponaria vaccaria.* This is very similar to baby's breath, but pink. It is available from some of the English seed houses (such as Sutton's). Its sturdy stems will reach two-and-a-half feet, and the flowers make a pleasing contrast with the white baby's breath in bouquets.

Another annual for spring flowers that can be grown in flats is the blue lace flower, *Trachymene caerulea,* which has blossoms similar to Queen Anne's lace. All of these annuals can be grown in flats with several sowings to extend the cutting season.

Nemesia makes a charming cut flower when grown in four-inch pots. Seed should be sown in seed trays in August,

Most flowers grown for cutting thrive in a cool greenhouse.

transplanted into small pots when several leaves appear, and then potted up into the finishing pots. It will flower from January until March if grown in cool and sunny situations. The colors, which range from white to yellow and red are vibrant, making very pleasing small arrangements. Their stems will usually vary from six to 12 inches. A second sowing in December will produce flowers from April until June. *Nemesia* 'Blue Gem,' available from Sutton's, is a particularly noteworthy variety with small flowers that range in hue from dark blue to a blue so pale it is nearly white.

Another small flower suited to growing in four-inch pots is *Linaria.* 'Northern Lights' is a recommended variety available from most catalogs. Grown from seed started in August in seed trays and later transplanted into small pots before being moved into four-inch containers, it will start to flower in November and continue until May. The flowers, which come in a wide range of colors, are like very tiny snapdragons and are produced on thin, delicate stems that need support either with bamboo stakes and strings, or branched twigs from shrubs.

If you can plant starters directly in the benches of your greenhouse, you can produce a good crop of calendulas for cutting. Calendulas do best in a very cool, sunny house. Seed should be sown in August (use the tallest varieties available), transplanted into small pots, and then planted into the bench. Since they will flower for three to four months, give them at least ten inches between plants. The first flowers should appear in October or November and will be largest if the side buds are pinched off each stem as the buds begin to enlarge. Whitefly can be a problem with calendulas, but constant attention will keep that pest under control.

When grown cool, given support and planted in the benches, annual candytuft will produce tall, strong stems carrying large, flat clusters of white, pink or red flowers. The large whites are the most popular florist's variety, but the white/pink/red bedding plant mixes (such as 'Fairy Mix') also produce charming cut flowers. Seed can be sown in trays in January, transplanted into small pots, then planted directly into the greenhouse bench where they should flower in May. Earlier or later sowings provide a somewhat longer blooming season, but June weather renders the greenhouse too hot for these cool-loving early cut flowers.

Godetia makes an outstanding cut flower. Seed is sown in January in trays, transplanted into small pots and then planted in a bench in March. In fact, you might try planting godetias in the calendula bench after that crop has been pulled. 'Sybil Sherwood,' available from Sutton's, is a popular variety with lovely salmon and white flowers. Though the petals of godetia appear to be delicate and easily bruised, the flowers continue to open over a long period of time. Damping-off and other soil diseases can be a problem with godetias, but starting with a sterile seed-sowing medium and careful attention to watering, ventilation and temperature will give good control.

Ammi is a charming white flower borne in large flat clusters very similar to Queen Anne's lace. If seed is sown in January, then transplanted into small pots before benching in March or April, flowers may be expected in May. *Ammi* must have plenty of support, as the plants can easily reach five feet. Equally suitable and requiring similar cultivation techniques are bachelor's buttons and sweet sultans. If treated like *Ammi*, they reach an equally tall height and will flower until hot weather arrives in later spring.

Two old-fashioned favorites for wintertime cut flower bouquets are buddleia and stevia. These two must be grown from cuttings rather than seed. Stevia (*Piqueria trinerva*) has tiny white flowers that are sweetly fragrant. *Buddleia asiatica* has long slender spikes of fragrant white flowers while *Buddleia officinalis* has shorter spikes of fragrant lavender flowers. Cuttings can be taken in March or April and grown in pots either in the greenhouse or outdoors in a cold frame during the summer. Occasional feeding and pinching will produce healthy, bushy plants. Before frost threatens, they must be brought into a sunny, cool greenhouse (45 degrees F is sufficient) where they will flower. Although these cut flowers are otherwise easy to grow, they are prone to attacks by whitefly.

Many bulbs are ideal for growing in a cool greenhouse, particularly if you have a cold frame or root cellar available for storage, or a spot outdoors where the flats or pots of bulbs can be buried under peat moss or sand. Tulips, hyacinths, crocus and narcissus are familiar to all gardeners. However, indoor gardeners should also experiment with iris, freesias, ornamental onions, ornithogalums and lilies. As with all bulbs to be used for forcing, the grower should purchase the largest and best quality bulbs available.

The florist's iris are easy to care for as long as good ventilation is available. Iris bulbs that are not prepared for forcing should be placed in a four-inch-deep wooden flat and stored in a cold frame for several months to allow good root growth before being brought into the greenhouse. If the bulbs are "flatted" in November, they are usually ready to be brought into the greenhouse by February or March. Bulbs that have been prepared for forcing can be flatted and put into the greenhouse immediately. Be careful with your watering, allow space between the flats for extra air circulation, and do not move the flats once the buds are showing. Any damage to the roots may cause the buds to blast. Blue or white iris are usually the best varieties for forcing under glass; the yellows tend to have weak stems when grown indoors.

Freesias do not require any special handling before planting in the greenhouse. In addition, staggered planting throughout the winter will give you a long season of bloom. The most satisfactory flowers will be produced in cool greenhouses with bright light. Freesias can be planted either in pots or in the bench. In either case, staking is necessary to prevent the foliage and flowers from flopping. Not only are freesias easily grown, but their bright colors and fragrant flowers are favorites during the cold months of the year.

Ornamental onions are also attractive and easily grown. *Allium moly* has a small yellow flower perfect for arrangements. The white *A. neapolitanum* or the improved *A. cowanii* are even nicer as cut flowers. Their bulbs are simply pressed into the surface of the soil and placed in a cool greenhouse. Bulbs planted in November and grown at 50 degrees F nighttime temperatures will usually flower in February and March. A more carefree bulb for greenhouse forcing is hard to find.

Ornithogalum arabicum is a fascinating plant in the lily family. The white flowers, each one and a half to two inches across with a black pistil in the center, are held in clusters at the top of strong one-and-a-half- to two-and-a-half-foot tall stems. Ornithogalum bulbs can be grown individually in four-inch pots or planted together in flats. A root-forming period in a cold frame or a cool, protected spot should precede their placement in the greenhouse where they will flower. At 50 degrees F nighttime temperatures, they will usually flower in March and April, although they can be coaxed into bloom earlier if grown at 60 degrees F.

Lilies are spectacular flowers that can be grown during late winter and spring to make large, colorful arrangements for the house. They are relatively easy to force in a cool greenhouse, provided you begin with precooled bulbs, sterile soil and clean pots, and do not overwater. The lilies most commonly used for forcing are the Asiatic hybrids such as 'Enchantment' (red-orange), 'Connecticut King' (yellow) or 'Firebrand' (red), though many others are available. For forcing, several bulbs are planted three to four inches deep in a large pot. If precooled bulbs are planted in December, flowers can be cut in March. Planting a few bulbs every three to four weeks will provide cutting material over several months of spring. 🌱

Oncidiums growing in the greenhouse at Planting Fields, Long Island, New York.

THE ORCHID GREENHOUSE

Charles Marden Fitch

When orchids are to occupy most of a greenhouse, the interior design must accommodate these unique tropicals. I find most orchid growers enjoy having a collection of many genera. My own collection contains genera from around the world; their mixing is successful when each orchid is placed according to its special needs.

Layers

In a typical orchid-region of tropical Asia or Latin America, orchids grow in three major levels. On the ground, in deep leafmold or on mossy rocks, terrestrials such as *Paphiopedilum* and *Anoectochilus* grow in low light while reed-stem *Epidendrum* and *Eria* thrive in sun.

Higher up, on tree trunks, steep rocky banks or tree crotches, live many showy genera such as *Oncidium* and *Phalaenopsis*. Finally, on fully exposed rocks, tree-

CHARLES MARDEN FITCH, *Mamaroneck, NY, an international horticulturist and media specialist, studies orchids in their tropical habitats around the world. He is author/photographer of many books including* **Garden Photography** *and* **All About Orchids**, *and guest editor of several* **Plants & Gardens** *handbooks.*

tops and sunny limb tips dwell orchids that need maximum light and excellent air circulation. These include species of *Ascocentrum*, some *Laelia*, *Vanda* and *Schomburgkia*.

Top to Bottom

I adapt this natural multi-level approach to habitat to fill available space top to bottom in the greenhouse. Hanging from the rafters are orchids that need maximum light. Under the highest hanging post are those of younger orchids and genera that do well with less-intense light. On the greenhouse bench are seedlings and orchids that will bloom with the dappled light that gets through the canopy above.

Orchids need more intense light than many other popular ornamental tropicals. When you have a choice about greenhouse placement, always select an orientation with maximum sun exposure, then control intensity with shade paint, rolling shade cloth or blinds.

In my lean-to greenhouse, a wall of the house blocks the sun after mid-afternoon. As it gets less than maximum sun, I supplement the natural light with fluorescent lights. To better grow orchids against this inside wall I hang fluorescent fixtures with broad-spectrum lamps over the plants.

Under the benches I put more fluorescent fixtures so orchids can actually be grown from the floor level on up to the roof glass level. Without the supplemental fluorescent light under the inside benches, very little would grow well. Under the outside (lighter) bench one might grow terrestrial jewel orchids or similar orchids with low-light requirements. In my situation I'd rather have the flexibility of growing many genera under the benches, even though it means a higher electric bill.

Multi-Story

Some orchid growers use a two-story greenhouse if room permits. By constructing a spiral staircase and an overhead walkway, one can build a two-story greenhouse where hanging orchids fill the top story. Below, growers can create conventional raised benches at waist height. This sort of design permits many plants to fit inside a greenhouse although the actual ground footage is limited.

With this approach it is most important to have adequate air circulation. I have several small fans operating 24 hours per day, circulating the air but not blowing it directly at orchids. Aim a fan up at the roof, against a wall, or at the floor. One of my humidifiers also has a fan that goes on low speed all the time, then switches to high speed when the mist comes on.

Another way I get air circulation in a lean-to greenhouse is by using a small muffin fan to blow warm air from the house basement into the greenhouse, slightly above floor level. The air in my basement is warm because that's where the natural gas furnace, water heater, and washing machine are located. In cold weather the air helps heat the greenhouse. In warm months the basement is usually cooler than outside so the same system helps keep the greenhouse cool.

Micro-Climates

Since my favorite orchids like an intermediate to warm greenhouse (usually above 60 degrees F at night), I use micro-climates to accommodate genera that do best with cooler nights. For example *Odontoglossum* spp. grow well for me if I keep them under an outside bench where the air goes down to about 50 degrees on cold winter nights. Orchids that do best with warm nights, for example *Ascocenda* spp., thrive when I hang them at the end of the greenhouse nearest the heaters. Use a maximum-minimum thermometer to find micro-climates. Here are some orchid greenhouse details adapted from my book *All about Orchids*:

Shading

Some form of shading is often needed during summer months. Inexpensive shade paint compounds are used by many commercial growers but are rather messy for home use. I prefer to diffuse hot summer sun with frosted fiberglass panels above the greenhouse roof. Greenhouse supply firms and many orchid nurseries also sell shading fabric in various mesh sizes to give different percentages of shade. For example, a collection of mainly phalaenopsis orchids would need more shade protection than one of vandas or cymbidiums.

A modern way to share orchids is by electronically-operated roller blinds that come down over the greenhouse roof or roll out under the glass above the plants as temperatures rise. Such electric controls work well on thermostats so orchids can be left alone with no fear that they will burn if a cloudy spring day suddenly turns sunny.

Humidity

Most orchids do best with 50 to 60 percent humidity. The orchid greenhouse should have an efficient humidifier attached to a main waterline for automatic operation. Place the humidifier so that its mist or fog has several feet of free air space before it hits the plants. Orchids too close to a humidifier may be kept too wet for their health.

Another way to increase humidity, useful on dry windy days, is to soak the floor and mist the plants. I like to use a sturdy metal watering wand called "FoggIt." The "FoggIt" comes with two nozzles. The fine mist is good for lightly wetting plants on bright mornings while the coarser nozzle is excellent for soaking the roots or wetting the floor.

In the cold weather when my "Southern Burner" natural gas stoves are working almost constantly I put a metal baking pan filled with water over each stove. As the water heats it evaporates, thus adding to the humidity.

Heating

My greenhouses are heated by natural gas "Southern Burners." One model is vented through the roof via a three-inch stovepipe. Orchid buds blast easily in polluted air so vented heaters are best for orchid greenhouses. In another greenhouse I have a non-vented, open-burner heater but the orchids still thrive since fresh air is constantly introduced to the greenhouse through floor vents and the basement-to-greenhouse fan described earlier.

Electric heat is efficient and safe for orchids but too expensive and unreliable in my area of the Northeast. If I were to build a greenhouse from the ground up, I would use only vented natural gas heaters or a hot-water system with the water heated in a natural gas burner.

Air Cooling

Air cooling is required for greenhouses when outside temperatures are high. Sun beaming through the glass or plastic will heat up interiors very rapidly, a good thing in cold weather but dangerous for plants if temperatures get too high. Most orchids can survive summer days of 90 to 100 degrees F as long as humidity keeps pace with the heat. Relative humidity *drops* as temperatures rise so in hot sunny weather the humidifiers will be a great help in protecting plants. Having adequate vents is also good. I like automatic roof vents that open when inside temperatures reach 85 degrees F.

In parts of the country where summers are not too humid, orchid growers use evaporative coolers to lower greenhouse temperatures. Dry outside air is drawn over a wet fiber mat by a big fan. As the air goes through the wet fibers it is cooled and humidified. This system works well in areas like Southern California but isn't efficient where outside air is humid. Growers in the Northeast often use regular air conditioners to help their orchids get through summer heat waves.

Summer Vacation

The hundreds of orchids in my greenhouses are too crowded so I give them a summer vacation outdoors. When the warm weather stabilizes I move many of them outside, where they live under tall oak trees until September. Cool-growing orchids are the first to go out and the last to be brought in. *Dendrobium nobile* hybrids and standard *Cymbidium* orchids require fall nights in the 50's if they are to bloom well. I leave these types outside until just before a frost. Warmer growers come in by early September.

Some orchid growers have sun-rooms or greenhouses where one or more walls can be opened up in warm weather. This system, along with putting plants outdoors, works where summers are humid but would not be good where humidity is below 50 percent.

Commercial and home orchid growers differ in the way they use greenhouses. The commercial growers frequently fill a greenhouse with one or two genera, the plants being neatly spaced on raised, ventilated benches.

In contrast, the home orchid grower fills a greenhouse to overflowing, usually with a well-diversified assortment of genera. This is a good idea since a multi-genera collection can have something in

An array of cattleyas shows their many forms and colors. Their striking flowers are long lasting.

bloom every day of the year. The disadvantage to this year-round love of beauty is a jammed greenhouse.

My final suggestion, from one who admits to having an overcrowded collection, is to build a greenhouse double the size you THINK is adequate. In a few seasons you will be pleased to have the space. 🌱

A SCHEDULE FOR GROWING CUT FLOWERS IN THE GREENHOUSE

JAMES STEVENSON

WITH ASSISTANCE FROM

DEBORAH MATTHEWS

Just as a garden should be designed on paper before applying spade to soil, a plan for producing cut flowers over a long season is equally important. To create a successful schedule for forcing cut flowers, consider the numbers of plants, seedlings or bulbs needed, and the area of bench or bed available.

A schedule is particularly important when forcing bulbs. Try to plan as much of your yearly bulb-growing needs as possible on paper before starting the project. Look through bulb catalogs for ideas of what varieties are available. Bulb suppliers will not be anxious to spend time answering your questions in September or October when they are over-extended. They are often happy to help, however, if contacted during the summer when their business is slow. They can give advice on how best to put together an order that fits your individual needs, including the scheduling of delivery dates scattered throughout the season for various planting times. Be sure to discuss shipping methods, especially if you plan mid-winter deliveries. Not all carriers can ensure the fast service necessary to prevent frozen shipments.

Starting in the spring, an unheated, plastic-covered frame house can be used to produce a great variety of cut flowers from early April until late June. After that date, you can rely on outdoor plantings of annuals and perennials to yield flowers for the house. A frame house can be made with metal pipes or wood, constructed over fertile ground, and the flowers grown directly in the soil.

The frame house provides minimal protection. It allows you to put plastic over the bed, extending the growing season by providing some protection from frost, wind and rain. A curved-top frame house is better than a square design for this purpose because there will be less damage to the plastic from ice and snow. Posts set into the ground around the perimeter of the bed permit supports to be put up for the taller growing flowers, such as snapdragons.

Bulbs and tubers such as tulips, anemones, ranunculus and florist's iris can be planted in the ground in October or November. At this time the plastic covering is not necessary. However, it will be required for spring crops, and is more easily installed in the fall. Cutting from bulbs will begin in April for anemones and tulips and continue in May for iris and ranunculus.

Once danger of hard frost is past,

74

seedlings that have been started indoors and hardened off outdoors can be planted in another section of the frame house, usually in mid-to late-March.

Some crops which can be successfully grown this way are stocks, snapdragons, bachelor's buttons, calendula, larkspur, annual scabiosa, matricaria and annual chrysanthemums ('Eastern Star' is an old favorite and a good producer). These seeds should be sown in seed trays in January or February; they can be transplanted into small plastic pots or peat pots when several true leaves have appeared. Peat pots can be transplanted directly into the soil bed in the plastic house. However some plants, such as snapdragons, resent being transplanted into peat pots.

The quality of the cut flower plants grown under plastic, and left unheated in the early spring, is often better than the same plants grown outdoors later in the season. Each produces best under cool growing conditions, and the plastic covering will protect the flowers from all weather damage except a late, hard frost.

Watering, occasional fertilizing, staking or other support, venting when the temperatures rise, and watching for aphids are all crucial factors in producing good cut flowers. The plastic house must be checked everyday for watering and venting. A grower will experience the best results if he keeps the house open as much as possible. An occasional feeding with a water-soluble fertilizer will keep your plants growing.

If supports are necessary for your crop, it is a good practice to erect the supports when the seedlings are set into the ground. Open wire mesh or plastic mesh is very efficient and easy to put into place. It can be purchased in three-foot or four-foot wide strips and stretched over cross-bars above the planting bed. Some of the taller plants may require a second or third layer of this support.

Scratching the soil with a cultivator every few weeks, or mulching with black plastic, will keep the weeds under control—this is necessary to ensure the healthiest flower-producing plants.

In spring, as the temperatures rise, you should cut more air vents in the plastic. By June it may be necessary to remove the plastic entirely.

In mid- to late-June, when outdoor beds are beginning to produce, the plants inside the frame house can be pulled out and discarded or put on the compost pile. Soil should be improved for the next crop of flowers, which might include tall mums planted in July for cutting in October and November. Before the first frost arrives in fall, cover the frame with new plastic to protect the mums. When they have ceased to flower, or have been finished by a hard frost, prepare the bed for early spring bulbs.

With experience you can enjoy cut flowers in your greenhouse over a long period of time by carefully scheduling seed-sowing dates, planting and flowering dates, and removal dates. Chrysanthemums, snapdragons, and paperwhite narcissus will yield cut flowers in the fall. Calendulas, stevia, buddleia, snapdragons, stocks, nemesia and linaria flower during the midwinter months. Bulbs such as ornamental onions, lilies, tulips, narcissus, iris, freesias and godetia, baby's breath, ammi, centaureas and candytuft will flower in early spring. For later spring flowering, all of the plants in the unheated plastic house will yield lovely flowers for bouquets.

One last word of advice—keep records of the year's activities such as seed sowing, transplanting, benching or flatting dates, first and last cutting dates, spacing and numbers of plants or bulbs used. All of this information will be invaluable for scheduling the following year's cut flowers.

PLANT PROPAGATION

BOB WEIDNER

The propagation of plants is a source of great pleasure for plant lovers. Nothing quite equals the joy of producing new plants. From start to finish, propagation is the product of your own skill and efforts.

Plant propagation is a vast topic, and professionals employ many different techniques—too many to discuss in a short article. To give you some idea of the diversity of propagation techniques, Volume I of Bruce MacDonald's *Practical Plant Propagation* has no less than 634 pages devoted to the subject. Let us limit ourselves to rooting vegetative cuttings in the home or small greenhouse. Anyone who truly enjoys gardening should not hesitate to try his hand at this method of reproducing plants.

When propagating plants in the home, it is important to start with the right attitude. Do not expect 100 percent success with your cuttings. Rooting even a few cuttings on your first try should be considered a "success". At each attempt, you will get a little better. Concentrate on your successes and forget the failures.

As in every aspect of gardening,

preparation and planning gives the most successful results. First, one must prepare the structure in which the cuttings will be rooted. There are innumerable types in use.

The best structure is a small greenhouse equipped with three-foot-high benches. It should have an intermittent mist system over each bench, with mist lines which can be valved off in several sections. It should be shaded down to

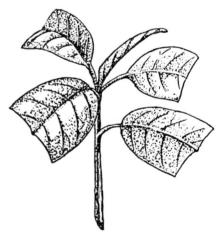

Large leaves can be clipped to about half size to allow more cuttings per unit of area and to reduce surfaces from which the cuttings can lose excessive water.

ILLUSTRATIONS BY PETER NELSON

BOB WEIDNER *of Leucadia, CA studied under T.H. Everett at the New York Botanical Garden and was past president of the Western Division of the International Plant Propagator's Society. He was the owner of Weidners' Begonia Gardens, Inc.*

2000 foot candles, measured midday on a bright day. An easy test is to move your hand back and forth over the surface of a bench on a bright day at noon. If the light is correct, you should almost but not quite be able to see the shadow of your hand.

Second best is a polyethylene tunnel house. There are unlimited designs of these houses and they can be put to a variety of uses. My favorite design is quickly constructed. Have a piece of ground levelled 12 feet wide and as long as you wish your house, up to 21 feet long. At the 10 foot mark, lay two 1" x 12" boards lengthwise ten inches apart and fasten them upright with stakes driven into the ground. Place 20-foot plastic pipes every five feet, bend them into hoops and attach to the 1" x 12" boards. Then cover this frame with polyethylene sheets. The plastic sheets are fastened to the 1" x 12" boards with laths and six-penny nails.

The leaves on lower third of cutting are removed.

The open ends are then covered with a plastic sheet fastened at the top and rolled up on an 11-foot piece of 1"x3" wood. This will allow a walk-in space for cleaning and also for venting when the house gets warmer than 85 degrees F. The entire tunnel should be shaded to 2000 foot candles measured on a bright day at noon.

To further prepare your structure, spray the empty house and ground with a strong clorox spray. You will need to use two inches of one-quarter inch crushed rock on the ground to keep your flats off the soil. Finally, install two mist lines controlled by a time clock for even misting.

Both of these structures are for the serious home propagator. But the same theories can be scaled down for the small house propagator. Very small "mini-greenhouses" can be purchased. Or a very small plastic tunnel house can be made just as easily as a large one. Simply bear in mind that the reason for any greenhouse propagating structure is to increase the humidity in the air so that the cutting will not dry out before it has made roots. Even a single pot can be made into a mini-greenhouse. Insert your cuttings, water them and cover the miniature greenhouse by placing a clear plastic bag over the top and fastening it around the rim of the pot.

Next you must provide a rooting medium. It should be lightweight, well-drained and evenly mixed. A mixture of sand and peat is often used, and vermiculite and peat is also popular. But both these mixes tend to hold more water than the ideal medium; and retained water tends to promote decay on the basal end of the cutting. Instead I would recommend peat moss and perlite, in even amounts. Add Osmocote time-release fertilizer at three to four pounds per cubic yard. For convenience sake, prepare enough so you can use it on other occasions. Use a shovel or a small cement mixer to get a thorough mixing.

Take a metal container such as a roasting pan and fill it with soil. Insert a meat thermometer into the center of the soil mass and place it in the oven. Raise the

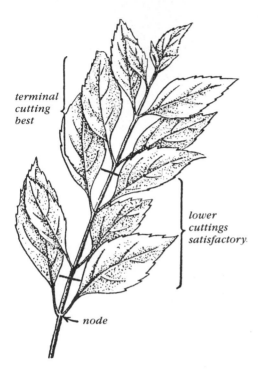

terminal
cutting
best

lower
cuttings
satisfactory

← node

Terminal sections are best for softwood
cuttings but long shoots can be cut
into several sections.

temperature to 160 degrees F and hold it
there for one-half hour; then let it cool.
If it is too dry, moisten it lightly. The balance of the soil should be put in a large
plastic bag, tied tightly and stored until
needed.

Next we must think of tools, containers and materials. A very sharp knife and
pruning shears are essential. Dull knives
and shears tend to crush cuttings.
Knives, shears and all other tools should
be sterile. In the case of scarce and valuable plants, it is often wise to run knives
and shears over an alcohol flame. For
less crucial work, a dip in strong clorox
suffices. A dibble to make holes for
inserting cuttings is an aid, but a common lead pencil will do the job if only a

few cuttings are being made. For larger
lots, a pointed piece of dowel rod one-
quarter by eight inches does a good job.

A hose with a mist nozzle or fine rose
nozzle to water-in cuttings is essential. In
addition, some nursery flats (the quantity depends on how many cuttings you
wish to make) are the best containers.
Again, they must be clean. A handy way
to sterilize flats is to put a piece of
polyethylene sheeting on the ground,
place the flats on it, then bring up the
sides and tie them to form a tank. Fill the
tank with a mix of the ratio of 1:10
clorox to water, being sure to cover the
flats. After ten minutes the flats will be
sterile. Be careful not to reinfect them.

Next fill the flats with empty two or
two-and-one-half inch plastic, clay or peat
pots. These are then filled with sterile
soil. By this method, you will have a plant
with an intact ball of roots and soil, ready
to continue growing on with the least
amount of shock.

Having accomplished all of this preparation, you are ready to begin the actual
cutting. It is very important to carefully
select cutting wood. Why bother to multi-
ply a plant with poor color, bad form or
no vigor? Select a plant that has sufficiently mature growth, but not hard
wood. Hard wood cuttings are another
class, not to be confused with this section. We want wood that is beginning to
firm up. But, in most cases, cuttings
should be made before flower buds
form. Many plants with flowers will root,
but they usually make weaker growth as a
result. Other plants, such as impatiens
and begonias, only develop flowering
growth and will not become bushy plants
if cuttings are taken in the full blooming
stage.

Take your cuttings just below the first
or second fully opened leaf, and cut off
that bottom leaf. To prevent infection,
no leaf should be touching the soil when
inserted. If a mass of leaves are crowded

at soil level, it is an invitation for Botrytis and other serious diseases.

If you are taking a large quantity of cuttings, be sure to keep them moist by placing them in the greenhouse under mist or in the shade and covered with a wet sheet of newspaper before insertion.

You will need two dipping materials, one to speed rooting and one to help prevent disease. Rootone or Hormodin may be put in a shallow saucer. However, many gardeners do not realize that powdered rooting hormones lose their strength with time. Store them in a refrigerator!

A fungicidal dip is made up of two teaspoons of Benomyl (Benlate) to one gallon of water. Five or ten cuttings, depending on size, can be gently swished around in the dip for a few moments, immersing the entire cutting in the solution. Then remove the cuttings and shake off the surplus liquid. Next, dip the tip of the cutting in the rooting powder, tapping off the surplus powder back into the dish.

Make holes for the cuttings with your dibble and insert the cuttings, firming them gently with your fingers. Then use your misting nozzle to thoroughly water-in the flat and place it in the misting tunnel.

Set the timing of your intermittent mist at approximately four to five seconds every ten minutes. And watch carefully for a few days to see if the interval of mist is sufficient but not too frequent. The mist need not be on at night, unless your heating system dries the air excessively.

Check the cuttings daily for the first few weeks and remove any dead or dying leaves. If there are any signs of disease, clean the affected plants and spray them with Benlate.

By the end of the fourth week, rooting should be achieved and the plants can be removed from the excessively moist con-

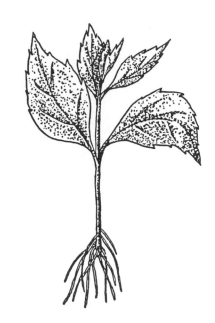

Rooted cutting ready for transplanting.

ditions. Allow them to become accustomed to the drier air for a week or two. When the pot is well filled with roots and your small plant is growing vigorously, you are ready to pot it on into the next larger size pot.

There are other ways to propagate plants vegetatively. For example, dieffenbachias and dracaenas can be propagated by cutting their long, bare stems into segments. The stems are cut into two-and-one-half-inch-long pieces, and each piece must have an "eye" which shows as a little bump on the stem and ensures that the piece will sprout new growth. Place the pieces horizontally in a flat in the same basic peat perlite soil mix, taking care always to position the eye facing straight up. Keep the soil continually moist, and pot up the segment as soon as the eye begins to grow.

Ficus plants present another problem because the milky sap tends to harden and it prevents the plant from taking up water. The best method of propagation is

79

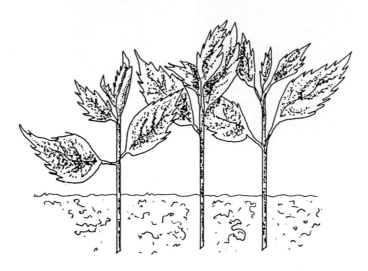

Cuttings are inserted into the medium to one-half of their length.

to air-layer this plant. In order to make a successful air-layer, it is essential to use a very sharp knife. You will also need a small stake (a quarter-inch by eight-inch dowel works admirably), some durable string and two handfuls of very wet sphagnum moss.

At a point at least eight inches from the top of the plant, cut or break off a leaf. Holding the eight-inch dowels as support against the stem, cut an upward slant behind the incision, but take care not to cut more than half way through, always holding the dowel rod as support. Keep the cut slightly ajar and place a little sphagnum in the opening to keep the wound open in order to prevent healing. Tie the dowel rod against the stem above and below the cut. Then place two handfuls of wet sphagnum as a ball around the wound. Finally, wrap the ball of sphagnum in one thickness of plastic. You will be able to see the roots through the plastic as they grow. When the layer is well-rooted, cut it off below the wound, pot it up and place it in a plastic tent for about a month until it is well established.

When you have mastered these methods of propagation you can be justifiably pleased with yourself. Brag a bit to your friends. But be prepared for the next batch of cuttings to fail completely! 🍃

80

DISEASE PROBLEMS IN HOME GREENHOUSES

ROBERT L. WICK

The Causes of Plant Disease

The causes of plant diseases are diverse and include pathogenic microorganisms as well as non-living factors such as air pollution, nutritional imbalances and other environmental stresses. For the purpose of

DR. ROBERT WICK *received his PhD in plant pathology from Virginia Polytechnic Institute and State University. He is an assistant professor and runs the plant diagnostic laboratory at the University of Massachusetts Waltham Suburban Experiment Station.*

this article, only diseases caused by fungi, bacteria, viruses and nematodes that are common to greenhouses will be covered. It should be noted that most microorganisms are not capable of causing plant diseases but rather perform important functions including contributing to soil formation, releasing nutrients from organic matter and suppressing plant pathogenic microorganisms.

Fungi are filamentous in structure and grow over or through the substrate that provides them with nutrition. Those

Slug damage on a *Phalaenopsis* orchid flower. PHOTO BY CHARLES MARDEN FITCH

that have evolved into plant pathogens attack living plants, causing loss of food or aesthetic value. Fungi are extremely diverse in their ecology, growth habits, form and pathogenicity. Symptoms of disease also vary and include root rot, canker, leaf spot, abnormal growth and wilt.

Fungi that survive and reproduce in the soil are termed soil-borne. They are the principal cause of root and crown (lower stem) rot. Soil-borne fungi generally do not produce air-borne spores but are easily transported from contaminated soil to pathogen-free soil by tools, hose ends, water splash and hands. Fungi that cause disease of stems, foliage and flowers usually produce spores that are easily disseminated by air currents or insects.

Bacteria are very small microorganisms that occasionally cause important plant diseases in greenhouses. To put their size into perspective, approximately 600 bacteria lined up end-to-end would span one-sixteenth of an inch. With few exceptions, they cause disease by colonizing the internal tissues of plants, thereby interrupting normal growth and function. Like fungi they cause soft rots, cankers, leaf spots, abnormal growth and wilt. Plant pathogenic bacteria are also diverse in their ecological and pathological attributes. Spread of bacteria is usually by splashing irrigation water, contaminated tools and hands and by propagating from diseased plants.

Viruses are ultramicroscopic infectious particles. They can reproduce only in the presence of living host cells. Infected plants often do not show symptoms and may inadvertently introduce viruses into the greenhouse. The most familiar symptoms, mosaics, ringspots, line patterns and yellowing of the veins occur on the foliage. Tobacco mosaic virus (TMV) and tomato spotted wilt virus (TSWV) are common on green-house plants and can infect many different hosts. TMV is spread by physically handling diseased and then healthy plants. Cigarettes often harbor TMV so don't smoke when handling susceptible plants. TSWV is spread by thrips which are very small insects that are difficult to detect. Other insects such as aphids and leafhoppers can also spread viruses. Controlling plant-feeding insects in the greenhouse will help reduce the incidence of virus diseases.

Nematodes are small (one thirty-second to one-quarter-inch long) round-worms that are common inhabitants of field soil. Most nematodes are not parasitic on plants but prey on micro-organisms, insects and other nematodes. Plant parasitic nematodes may attack the root system, stem or foliage depending on the species of nematode involved. Root-knot nematodes (*Melodogyne* spp.) cause galls of various sizes (usually one sixteenth to one-quarter inch) on the roots of a wide range of plants. The bulb and stem nematodes (*Ditylenchus* spp.) occur on hyacinth, narcissus, daffodil, tulip, and iris as well as other plants. Colonized bulbs may have necrotic areas and developing leaves have swellings and distorted growth. Foliar nematodes (*Aphelenchoides* spp.) attack the leaves and occur on bird's-nest fern, African violet, gloxinia, Rieger begonia, chrysanthemum, Boston fern, phlox, peperomia and India rubber plant. Symptoms caused by foliar nematodes may be easily mistaken for those caused by fungi or bacteria.

Plant Disease Control

Many diseases are not successfully controlled because the cause was not accurately determined. Thus, the first principle of disease control is to identify the cause of the problem. This may be done with the appropriate literature and experience but often technical help is necessary. Contact your local Cooperative Extension office, plant disease clinic or garden center for assistance.

The use of resistant cultivars (varieties) is the ideal way to control diseases. Vegetable seed is usually designated as resistant to *Verticillium, Fusarium,* and root-knot nematode (or V, F, and N respectively). Resistance to other pathogens is available but limited. Check with your seed supplier or catalog for resistant cultivars.

Sanitation and cultural practices are among the most important ways to prevent and control plant diseases. Sanitation is a general term for the removal of diseased plant material and for the surface disinfection of tools and working surfaces. When disease occurs, affected plants or plant parts should be removed and taken away from the greenhouse. Do not discard plant material under the bench. Plant litter should be periodically removed from the floor. Used pots, flats and tools should be washed free of soil and treated with a 1:9 Clorox:water solution. Metal surfaces should be rinsed with water after treatment with Clorox to prevent rusting. Wooden structures and flats can be treated with copper naphthalate.

Sound cultural practices include the use of a pathogen-free growing medium with desirable physical qualities for the crop to be grown, proper regulation of water, fertilizer, temperature and humidity, and proper planting techniques. A continual effort must be made to avoid recontamination of the growing medium. Soil-less media (peat/perlite/vermiculite and other nonsoil mixtures) do not have to be treated before use. However, a preventative application of one or more fungicides is desirable for plants that are prone to damping-off or root rot. Soil from out-of-doors, whether used by itself or as an amendment in a soil-less medium, must be treated to eliminate soil-borne plant pathogens, insects and weeds. Hose nozzles which contact the floor or other soiled surfaces can effectively contaminate the growing medium with root rot pathogens. Provide a hook on the wall to hang up the hose.

Overwatering displaces oxygen in the soil resulting in an unhealthy root system and at the same time providing favorable conditions for root rot organisms such as the fungi *Pythium* and *Phytophthora.* Also, when soil remains cold and wet, ammonium, which is a fertilizer constituent, can build up to toxic levels. Over-fertilization can directly damage roots and also increase the severity of *Pythium* root rot. Have the growing medium tested periodically for ammonium and soluble salt levels.

The avoidance of high humidity and condensation of water on plants is essential for controlling *Botrytis* blight as well as other foliar diseases. High humidity is most prevalent during spring and fall. As the sun sets, temperatures fall and the relative humidity increases until the dew point is reached. Humid, wet conditions provide an ideal environment for spore germination and infection of plant tissues. To reduce humidity, evacuate the air from the greenhouse to allow the cool night air to come in. Raise the temperature several degrees and the relative humidity will decrease. Proper spacing of plants on benches, watering in the morning and circulating air with fans will also help reduce humidity within the plant canopy and thus help reduce diseases. An humidistat is a wise investment.

Fungicides can provide excellent control of some diseases but for others they may be ineffective, unavailable or illegal. When purchasing and using fungicides one must know which fungi are to be controlled, whether the fungicide is labeled for greenhouse use and if it is the appropriate formulation for the application methods at hand. Do not rely on fungicides alone. A holistic approach to plant disease control is a much sounder approach.

Common Diseases in the Greenhouse

DAMPING-OFF

Damping-off is a disease of young seedlings caused by soil-borne fungi. Affected plants collapse and may have root rot, stem lesions at the soil surface or both. Flats of seedlings often damp-off in a circular pattern because fungi grow radially from the point of origin. Hot water from heat-baked pipes and hoses, excessively hot or cold temperatures and over-fertilization can mimic symptoms of damping-off. To control damping-off, it is essential to sow seeds in a pasteurized growing medium and to avoid overwatering and contamination with untreated soil. For particularly susceptible plants, use fungicide-treated seed or incorporate the appropriate fungicide into the medium at planting time.

ROOT ROT

Root rot is a destructive disease caused by several soil-borne fungi. Occasionally soft rot bacteria and plant pathogenic nematodes are involved. Healthy, actively growing feeder roots are white to light brown and firm. Diseased roots may have one or more of the following symptoms: water-soaked appearance, brown or black lesions, soft-rotting of the tissues and "rattailing," a condition where the outer cortex of the root sloughs off leaving a protruding resistant core (Fig. 1). Once above-ground symptoms of wilt occur, the disease has progressed too far and the plant cannot be saved. Since an unhealthy root system is not generally apparent until wilting occurs, every effort must be made to prevent root rot from occurring. Use a pathogen-free growing medium, avoid contamination

and apply water and fertilizer as needed. Fungicides can be used to protect particularly susceptible or valuable plants but they will not cure existing disease. Contact your local Cooperative Extension floriculture specialist for specific pesticide recommendations.

BOTRYTIS BLIGHT

Botrytis blight is caused by the fungus *Botrytis cinerea* and is one of the most important diseases in greenhouses. It can attack flowers, foliage and stems of a wide variety of plants. A characteristic sign of Botrytis blight is the appearance of a grey mold on the affected tissue. Optimum conditions for Botrytis spores to germinate and infect plants occur when the air temperature is 45 to 60 degrees F, free moisture is present on plant surfaces for eight to 10 hours and humidity is 93 percent or greater. Disease development and spore production are favored by temperatures between 68 and 75 degrees F. Botrytis blight is prevalent during spring and fall because that is when favorable conditions in the greenhouse are most likely to occur. Thorough sanitation will help to control Botrytis blight. Remove all plant debris and dead flowers. Heat and ventilate during periods of high humidity, space plants adequately and provide air circulation. Several fungicides are available for controlling this disease.

POWDERY MILDEW

Powdery mildew occurs on many different greenhouse plants and is especially important on begonia and rose. The disease is evident on the upper surface of the foliage as a white, mealy appearing deposit. The symptoms are the result of a crop of spores, which, on some hosts, may be fairly sparse and thus overlooked. Since the fungus only colonizes the upper layer of leaf cells, severe damage to the plant does not usually occur. An exception is begonia which can be severely damaged. The superficial growth habit of the fungus makes it one of the few diseases where application of the appropriate fungicide makes eradication possible.

BACTERIAL DISEASES

As mentioned earlier, bacteria can cause many different diseases with symptoms similar to those caused by fungi. Soft rot of corms, bulbs, rhizomes and cuttings is often caused by bacteria. Soft rot is evident by a mushiness of the affected tissues and often a foul-smelling odor. The disease usually occurs under conditions of excessive soil moisture. Wounding of tissues by improper handling or by insects can also be important. Cyclamen corms that are buried too deeply are subject to decay. Soft rot cannot be controlled with pesticides. Avoid wounding and overwatering.

Several bacterial blights occur on begonia, chrysanthemum, geranium, poinsettia and bedding and foliage plants. In some cases bacterial diseases are seed-borne or present when the plants were purchased. Some plant pathogenic bacteria may be permanent residents within the greenhouse. Bacterial blights are spread by handling diseased plants, splashing irrigation water and by vegetative propagation from diseased plants. Depending on the bacterium involved, it may eventually destroy the plant or it may be of a minor consequence. If the plant material is valuable, a diagnosis by a specialist should be made. To control bacterial blights, buy seed from a reputable source, inspect plants for lesions before bringing them into the greenhouse, remove diseased plants from the greenhouse and avoid wetting the foliage during irrigation. Bacterial blight cannot be effectively managed with pesticides.

Mites infesting an orchid leaf.
PHOTO BY CHARLES MARDEN FITCH

FUSARIUM AND VERTICILLIUM WILT

Fusarium and *Verticillium* are soil-borne fungi that cause vascular wilts of plants. Symptoms include leaf yellowing and wilting, often on one side of the plant. A cut into the stem base will often reveal a discoloration of the vascular tissue. *Fusarium* and *Verticillium* are not often a problem in greenhouses; however, they can be a problem when unpasteurized field soil is used to grow susceptible plants. Occasionally plants are purchased that have vascular wilt disease and symptoms may not show up for several weeks. Discard affected plants. Use a pasteurized growing medium.

85

AN ALTERNATIVE METHOD TO CHEMICALS: BIOLOGICAL CONTROL

L. J. DUPRE

Too often, we equate pest control with killing insects, but the purpose of pest control is to prevent the damage that insects cause and to preserve plant or crop quality.

When establishing your own program, it is crucial to understand how pest problems become epidemic. Study the relationship of H (Host), E (Environment) and P (Pest). The area where all three overlap is I (Infestation). Think of all three as dynamic.

Small areas of overlap by all three denote minor infestations; total or near total overlap means an epidemic and possible plant death. Pest control means manipulating H, E and P to eliminate or reduce I so any damage is tolerable.

An actively growing, healthy plant generally resists diseases and is not attractive to insects. Plants under stress are vulnerable to insect infestations. Plant stress may be caused by too much or too little water, air, heat, light, soil pH or incorrect fertilization. In addition, a greenhouse provides ideal conditions for pest growth and development. In that artificial environment, insects, diseases and weeds can proliferate.

If an insect problem arises, it is important to begin by identifying the cause. Examine the infested plant carefully. You will find a hand lens helpful for finding mites, small insects and eggs. Once you have identified the problem, you are ready to seek solutions.

An excellent place to begin is by calling your local Cooperative Extension Office listed in the phone book under "County Gov't." Horticultural Agents or trained Master Gardener volunteers on the staff will help you identify problems and offer advice on corrective measures. The following general suggestions might help to control infestations.

By far the simplest method of pest control is to exclude outdoor pests by covering your greenhouse vents with a fine mesh screen while also keeping the door closed or using a screen door.

Insects are attracted to bright yellow objects. Sticky yellow lures are very effective for catching winged, soft-bodied insects. Paint thin pieces of plywood (6" x 12") bright yellow, coat thinly with Tanglefoot, Tacktrap, petroleum jelly or oil and hang or stake near your plants. Clean and recoat the lure as needed.

L.J. DUPRE *of Anacortes, WA retired after 30 years in the U.S. Navy and then turned his talents to gardening. He has been a master gardener for 13 years and writes a weekly column for a local newspaper.*

Similar traps are often sold at garden centers.

Brewed coffee or tea also controls certain insects. However, the brew must have caffeine — decaffeinated beverages won't work.

Rubbing alcohol applied with a cotton swab or sprayed directly on the insect will help control mealybugs and scale insects.

Also effective are botanical preparations which include plant-derived poisons such as pyrethrins, rotenone, nicotine, ryania, sabadilla, and hellebore. They can be obtained locally or via mail order.

Both Safers, Inc., 60 William St., Wellesley, MA 02181 and Reuter Laboratories, Inc., 1400 Ford Building, Detroit, MI 48226 produce natural pesticides to control insects and diseases. Write to them for information and availability of their products.

Finely ground dusting sulfur is also relatively safe for controlling fungal diseases of plants.

Beneficial predatory or parasitic insects are available via mail order. Predators eat their prey while parasites lay their eggs in the eggs or bodies of other insects. Parasitic nematodes control damaging nematodes and insects which spend part of their life in the soil, although they do not harm earthworms. However, bear in mind that most beneficial insects are very specific about their host and so the pest to be controlled must be positively identified.

New botanicals are being tested and will shortly enter the supply pipeline. The neem tree (*Azadirachta indica*) of S.E. Asia has insecticidal properties and is being investigated. In addition, a broad spectrum insecticide derived from the American pawpaw tree has been patented. Beneficial molds to control disease problems have been isolated by USDA scientists.

Perhaps the most promising recent discovery is *Bacillus thuringiensis*. Almost 100 strains of this bacterial insecticide are being investigated as controls for a wide variety of insects including mites and beetles.

To keep abreast of developments in the field, look under "Biological Control" in the classified advertisement section of gardening magazines. 🍏

FOR FURTHER READING TRY:

Hussey, N.W. & Scopes, N.—editors. *Biological Pest Control, The Glasshouse Experience.* Ithaca, NY: Cornell University Press.

Cook, R. James and Baker, Kenneth F. *The Nature and Practice of Biological Control of Plant Pathogens.* American Phytopathological Society.

Ware, George W. *Complete Guide to Pest Control With and Without Chemicals.* Thomson Publications.

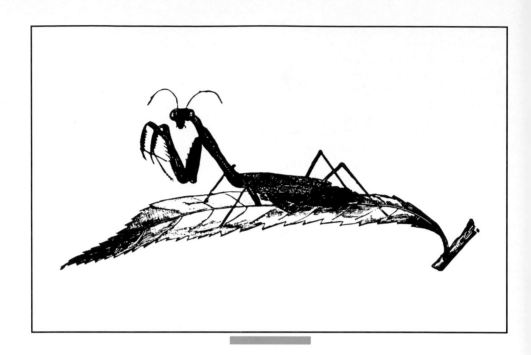

PUTTING BIOLOGICAL CONTROL INTO ACTION

ANNA EDEY

nsects have always been with us. Over 900,000 species are known to exist, and there may be twice that number not yet discovered. Approximately 99 percent of all insects are beneficial to mankind (insect-eaters, pollinators,

ANNA EDEY *of Martha's Vineyard, MA is the founder, designer and director of Solviva Winter Garden.*

aerators, composters, etc.). However, there are some insects that are considered to be harmful.

Since ancient times people have tried various methods of protection against insect infestations, but pests have remained a major problem all over the world. Solutions were sought in the form of chemical pesticides. However, we now

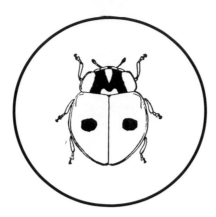

Lady beetle

know the disastrous consequences of relying on "miracle cures." Many people are seeking more lasting solutions which lie in developing an understanding of ecological balance and coexistence.

That is what I set out to do when I started my 3000-square-foot solar greenhouse, the Solviva Winter Garden, in 1983. I wanted to demonstrate the feasibility of producing abundant quantities and varieties of the highest quality vegetables, herbs and edible flowers year-round. And I wanted to accomplish this without causing pollution and depleting precious resources in a climate where the temperature can hover around 0 degrees F for days, and the sun can remain hidden for weeks. In addition, I wanted to demonstrate that this could be a financially viable business.

I am happy to report that after four years of continuously operating this solar greenhouse as an organic, high-yield year-round food garden, my hopes and dreams have not only been reached, but they have been greatly exceeded.

The solar operation is accomplished by combining sun's energy with animal heat. Sufficient heat is maintained throughout the winter by the storage of solar heat in about 4,000 gallons of water,

combined with the body heat of chickens and angora rabbits living in enclosures within the well-insulated greenhouse. The animals also provide manure compost for soil enrichment. No back-up heat is required, even in the worst weather conditions. Natural ventilation cools the greenhouse in summer without the need of electricity. Photovoltaic panels and batteries power the circulating fans and working lights.

In the solar greenhouse, the insect management is unusually effective, easy and low-cost. Most importantly, it is absolutely non-toxic. Here is an eight-point program for success:

1) Introduce and maintain a variety of beneficial insects some of which come in from outside (such as syrphid flies, chalcid wasps, tachinid flies and braconid wasps); combined with insects that are brought into the greenhouse (such as *Aphidoletes aphidimyza* — aphid parasite, praying mantis, etc.); and some insects that I order from Rincon-Vitova, an insectary in Oak View, California (such as *Encarsia formosa* — greenhouse whitefly parasite, ladybugs, lacewings, predatory mites, etc.).

2) Grow nectar-producing flowers such as dill, parsley, fennel, cilantro, and alyssum from which the beneficial insects

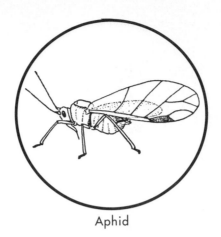

Aphid

draw supplemental nourishment.

3) I maintain maximum plant health by good management of soil, air, temperature, sanitation and harvesting in order to resist insect attacks. A healthy plant has a strong cell structure and is harder for insects to penetrate than a weak one.

4) I grow many nasturtiums as host plants. Not only are nasturtiums beautiful, edible and nutritious, but they thrive in the darker areas of the greenhouse where few other plants would be productive. Of all the 200 or so varieties of plants in the greenhouse, the nasturtiums are most attractive to aphids, whiteflies, thrips, spider mites and leafminers. Therefore, they also furnish excellent habitats for the beneficial predatory and parasitic insects.

5) I monitor the situation. While watering or harvesting I constantly check the ratio of "good guys" to "bad guys." When necessary, I take action to keep the situation in the proper balance.

6) I leave many insect infested plants standing. This principle is the most difficult for visitors to understand. However, the weakened plants will attract harmful insects more than their healthy neighbors. If I pulled plants as soon as they got pest infested, I would interrupt the reproductive cycle of many of the parasitic insects. Infested plants are important insectaries.

7) I trust that harmony will prevail. This means that I do not intervene to eradicate the "bad guys," not even with insecticidal soap. If an insecticide is meant to kill or harm, it would certainly do the beneficials equal damage either directly or as they interact with the poisoned pests.

8) I do some hand-picking and trapping. Slugs and caterpillars can be a nuisance, and are the only critters I spend any time controlling. Slugs are best hand-picked at dawn or dusk, or trapped in small containers pressed into the soil and filled with beer, or collected from rotting pieces of wood under which they hide during the day.

However, after four years of trying to control caterpillars by hand-picking with unsatisfactory results, I recently decided to use Dipel (*Bacillus thuringiensis*). Not only did it work well, but it is reputedly non-toxic to anything but leaf-eating caterpillars.

Occasionally, there are rushes of aphids, spidermites or whiteflies. I hang on, allowing some of the lettuce to be overcome by aphids, watching in suspense as the beneficials increase in

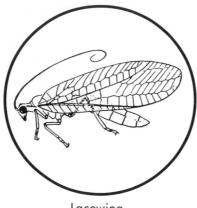

Lacewing

number. I go around with my magnifying lens and carefully distribute the beneficials to places in most need. As we harvest, we remove them and place them back in the greenhouse.

Research is rapidly progressing all over the world to find a biological control for every single pest, making it possible to achieve high food production without the use of any toxic chemicals. However, we are just beginning to discover the possibilities in biological control. There are some real challenges out there, not all of which are food related, such as wool moths, fleas, ticks and mosquitos.

Many people think of food crops as being riddled with pests which must be controlled with poisons. Therefore they assume that they cannot possibly grow foods in their home-attached greenhouses without endangering members of their household. The Solviva Winter Garden is living proof that it is possible to grow food safely in a greenhouse that is fully incorporated into a home. 🍃

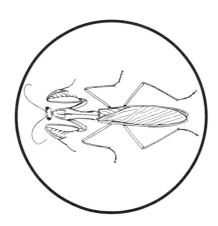

Praying mantid

SUPPLIERS OF BENEFICIAL ORGANISMS

This list of suppliers in North America is excerpted from a list by Larry Bezark and Helen Yee of the State of California Biological Control Services Program, 3288 Meadowview Road, Sacramento, CA 95832.

The following companies list several beneficial organisms that may be helpful to greenhouse growers:

Bio Insect Control
710 S. Columbia
Plainview, TX 79072

Harmony Farm Supply
P.O. Box 451
Graton, CA 95444
free catalog

King's Natural Pest Control
224 Yost Avenue
Spring City, PA 19475
free literature

Mellinger's Nursery
2310 W. South Range Road
North Lima, OH 44452

Natural Pest Controls
8864 Little Creek Drive
Orangevale, CA 95662

Necessary Trading Company
P.O. Box 603
New Castle, VA 24127
charge for catalog

Organic Pest Control Naturally
P.O. Box 55267
Seattle, WA 98155
charge for catalog

Peaceful Valley Farm Supply
11173 Peaceful Valley Road
Nevada City, CA 95959
free catalog

Rincon-Vitova Insectaries, Inc.
P.O. Box 95
Oak View, CA 93022
free brochure

GREENHOUSE MAGAZINES AND SOURCES

MAGAZINES

Reprinted by permission of the Indoor Citrus Society from the Summer 1987 issue of Indoor Citrus and Rare Fruit Society newsletter.

Greenhouse Grower—published monthly by Meister Publishing Co, 37841 Euclid Ave., Willoughby, OH 44094.

Greenhouse Manager—published monthly by Branchsmith Publishing, 120 St. Louis Ave., Ft. Worth, TX 76104.

Hobby Greenhouse—published by the Hobby Greenhouse Association, 8 Glen Terrace, Bedford, MA 01730.

GREENHOUSE SOURCES:

Below are companies that sell greenhouses, compiled from lists from *Hobby Greenhouse Magazine, Greenhouse Manager Buyers Guide* and Barbara Barton's book *Gardening by Mail.*

HOBBY GREENHOUSE:

Eden—Northwest Eden Sales, Inc., 15103 NE 68th St., Redmond, WA 98052

English Cottage Greenhouse—Smith & Hawken, 25 Corte Madera, Mill Valley, CA 94941

Santa Barbara Redwood—Charley's Greenhouse Supplies, 1569 Memorial Highway, Mount Vernon, WA 98273

Hoop House Greenhouse—Fox Hill Farm, 20 Lawrence St., Rockville, CT 06066

Sun-Lite Greenhouse—Solar Components Corp., P.O. Box 237, Manchester, NH 03105

Northern Light Greenhouse—Gardener's Supply Co., 133 Elm St., Winooski, VT 05404

Halls Greenhouse—W. Atlee Burpee Co., Warminster, PA 18974

GREENHOUSE MANAGER:
(M manufacturer, W wholesaler, D distributor.)

A&P Ag Structures (M), 11266 Ave. 264, Visalia, CA 93277.

ADJ Horti-Projects Inc.(M), Box 3004, Langley BC, Canada V3A 4R3.

Agro Projects (M), 7114 Pomelo Dr. I, Canoga Park, CA 91307.

Aluminum Greenhouses, Inc. (M), Box 11087, Cleveland, OH 44111.

Anderson Orchids, 2059 Lee Rd., Smyrna, GA 30080.

Atlas Greenhouses, 117 Wakefield, Hampton, CT 06517.

B.F.G. Supply Co. (W), 14500 Kinsman Rd., Burton, OH 44021.

Ball Seed Co., Box 335, W. Chicago, IL 60185.

Beck Greenhouse Co. (M), Box 650, Auburn, AL 36830.

Carson & Associates, Cliff, 204 Forest Dr., Greenwood, SC 29646.

Clover Greenhouses By Elliott Inc. (M.W.), Box 789, Smyrna, TN 37085.

D.A.C.E. Inc. (M), Box 475, Port Jefferson, NY 11776.

DeCloet Ltd. (M), Box 145, Tillsonburg, ON, Canada N4G 4H3.

Double A Truss Mfg. Co. Inc. (M.W.D), 320 Wetmore, Manteca, CA 95336.

Geiger Corp. (W.D), Rt. 63, Box 285, Harleysville, PA 19438.

Growers Intl. Inc. (W), Box 10, Schulenburg, TX 78956-0010.

Harnois Industries, (M.W) 1044 Main. St. Thomas of Joliette, PQ Canada, JOK 3LO.

Hydro-Gardens Inc., Box 9707, Colorado Springs, CO 80932.

Landreth Nursery Co., 1000 Far Shores, Hot Springs, AR 71913.

Lord & Burnham (M), Box 255, Irvington, NY 10533.

Ludy Greenhouse Mfg. Corp., Box 141, New Madison, OH 45346.

McAllister Co. Inc. (M.D.), Box 6667, Burbank, CA 91510.

Nexus Greenhouse Systems Corp. (M), 10983 Leroy Dr., Northglenn, CO 80233.

Northern Grower Systems Inc. (M), 1550 E. Shore Dr., St. Paul, MN 55106.

Pacific Coast Greenhouse Mfg. Co., 83600 Industrial Ave., Cotate, CA 94928.

Prins Greenhouses, 201 Maison St., Elmhurst, IL 60126.

Rough Bros. Inc. (M), Box 16010, Cincinnati, OH 45216.

Serac Ltd. (M), Box 2186, Davis, CA 95617.

Smith Inc. (M), Drawer X, Box 272, Red Bank, NJ 07701.

Stuppy, Inc., Box 12456, N. Kansas City, MO 64116.

V&V Noordland, Inc., Box 739, Medford, NY 11763.

VEBO Ltd. (M), 196 Belleview Ave., Center Moriches, NY 11934.

Van Wingerden Greenhouse Co., (M), 4078 Haywood Rd., Horse Shoe, NC 28742.

Vary Industries (M), Box 248, Lewiston, NY 14092-0248.

Winandy Greenhouse Co. Inc., 2211 Peacock Rd., Richmond, IN 47374.

Zethof Greenhouse Services Inc., Box 331, Wellington, OH 44090

(Check *Greenhouse Manager's* **All-Industry Buyer's Guide Product Directory**, Spring 1987, for additional manufacturers.)

GARDENING BY MAIL:

Gothic Arch Greenhouses, P.O. Box 1564, Mobile, AL 36633-1564.

House of Redwood, 2910 E. Blue Star Ave., Anaheim, CA 92806.

Santa Barbara Greenhouses, 1115 Ave. Acaso #J, Camarillo, CA 93010.

McGregor Greenhouses, 1195 Thompson Ave., Santa Cruz, CA 95062.

Machin Designs (USA) Inc., P.O. Box 167, Rowayton, CT 06853.

Bloomin' Greenhouse, Inc. 7591 Wilson Blvd., Jacksonville, FL 32210-3535.

Suncraft, Inc., 414 South Street, Elmhurst, IL 60126.

Janco Greenhouses, 9390 Davis Avenue, Laurel, MD 20707-1993.

Turner Greenhouses, P.O. Box 1260, Goldsboro, NC 27530-1260.

Sun System Greenhouses, 60-D Vanderbilt Motor Pkwy., Commack, NY 11725.

Four Seasons Greenhouses, 425 Smith Street, Farmingdale, NY 11735.

Vegetable Factory, Inc., 71 Vanderbilt Avenue, New York, NY 10169.

Aluminum Greenhouses, Inc., P.O. Box 11087, Cleveland, OH 44111-2140.

Cropking Greenhouses, P.O. Box 310, Medina, OH 44258.

Sturdi-Built Mfg. Co., 11304 S.W. Boones Ferry Rd., Portland, OR 97219.

Texas Greenhouse Co., 2723 St. Louis Ave., Ft. Worth, TX 76110.

Sunglo Solar Greenhouses, 4441 26th Ave. West, Seattle, WA 98199.